# Some Things Don't Change

# Some Things Don't Change:

*Enduring Principles from a Lifetime in Leadership and Sales*

Wayne B. Smith Jr.

©2023 copyright by Wayne B. Smith Jr.

Willow Oak Press

Charlotte, North Carolina

All photos and articles used with permission from The Toro Company.

ISBN: 978-1-0881-4801-3

## Dedication

For my wife, Indun Patrick.

To my daughters: Anna Lindsay Smith Yarbrough and Leigh Christian Smith Cooke.

To my grandchildren: Stokes and Taylor Yarbrough, and Smith, Covington, and Davis Cooke.

To my sister, Judy Smith Martin.

To my brother, Stephen E. Smith.

To Jonnie W. Smith.

For the employees of Smith Turf & Irrigation.

# CONTENTS

# PREFACE

I wanted a paycheck. Everybody else who worked there was getting a paycheck. During my first summer job when I was thirteen years old, I was getting $4 a week, but it was in cash, and it came in an envelope. The $4 a week did not bother me so much; what did bother me was that everyone else was receiving a printed check from the company with their name on it, and I was just getting $4 cash in an envelope. It was embarrassing. I knew, as did the others, that the cash came directly from Dad's pocket. I wanted to be like everyone else, not the boss's son who got special treatment.

My involvement with my family's distribution business began when I was a young kid, crawling all over the golf maintenance equipment at the company and the equipment on our farm, learning how to operate it, and hanging around the company office. Long before I had a driver's license, my dad had me working various jobs in the company, pulling and packing orders in the delivery department, working in the service department, and more.

Our family business sells outdoor power equipment and irrigation products for homeowners, landscapers, and golf courses. The business was founded by my grandfather in 1925 after the furniture company he was working for closed and he didn't have enough income to sustain his family. He went in search of work and came across a small manufacturing company called Toro. At that time, Toro had only a few products for golf course maintenance. Two weeks after talking to them, they called him back to the company and told him they were going to open a territory for their products for the southeastern United States, and asked if he wanted to be the distributor in that area for their products. He told them yes, and with his wife and their two boys, they packed their belongings in an old car and left Minneapolis for Jacksonville, Florida.

After a few years in Jacksonville, my grandfather was hit with another blow. This time by the Great Depression in the late 1920s. None of his customers were able to pay him, and all but one of his employees left because there was no money to pay them. In the early thirties, the country was beginning to recover from the Depression. Toro called to say they were going to add distributors in the Southeast, and he could stay in Florida or move to another territory. My grandfather's answer was: "There will never be anything in Florida." There's probably no way he could have ever anticipated the exponential growth of development in Florida.

He chose to move to Charlotte, North Carolina, with the two Carolinas as his territory. Although no one was able to pay him for previous sales in Florida, he never declared bankruptcy. He brought all of his bills with him to Charlotte, and over a number of years, paid every debt a little at a time. On Sunday afternoons, sitting on the floor, he and Dad opened the mail, and Granddad would put a few of the checks in a cigar box. I didn't know it at the time, but those cigar box checks were the ones he used to pay his previous bills from Florida. His integrity led him to believe everyone should be paid, regardless of the circumstance.

My summer work continued through my high school and college years. Dad moved me around to just about every job he could think of within the company. I did paperwork, drove trucks making deliveries, put equipment together, and helped the janitor clean the office. I spent two summers on the road as a sales representative between my years in college. I called on dealers selling outdoor power equipment. I called on boat dealers selling boats and outboard motors. I even spent one summer selling Titleist golf balls. The experience was priceless and more beneficial than I was able to appreciate at the time.

After college and a stint in the Air Force, I went to work for the company full time as a sales representative for golf course maintenance equipment. My six years of experience as a sales representative were probably as enjoyable as anything I have done in my career. I made great friends with my customers, their families, and even their pets.

I worked hard not only making sales, but also learning how to sell. I watched more experienced sales representatives, attended classes offered by companies, and read books on selling skills and techniques. I learned what made my customers tick, what was important to them, and how important personal relationships are to customers. I was excited about the opportunity to be a resource for my customers. It was flattering when they asked me for my help or even my opinion. Selling was even more fun with the friendly competition with the other salespeople in our company. I was the boss's son, and they loved to outsell me—and I loved the challenge of trying to outsell them.

After six years in sales, I had enough experience to become a sales manager. Now I was the boss of men who were older and more experienced. I believed I would probably be in that job until my dad decided to retire, even though I wasn't sure he would ever retire. (I like to refer to my jobs as "jobs," not positions, because that's what they were—jobs.) Once again, as sales manager, I'd been put in a position where I had a lot to learn.

How do you learn? You watch, listen, and apply yourself to what you learn. Each one of us is responsible for our own personal development, and the outcome rides on how much we really want to succeed. You can't lollygag around waiting on someone to drop success in your lap. That may happen occasionally, but not very often. You have to be intentional about it, because it takes discipline and work. It's not what you wish for, it's what you earn. When Michael Jordan was asked what he thought was his best skill, his answer was, "I was coachable. I was a sponge, and aggressive to learn." As the boss's son, all eyes were on me to see if I was up to the task. Of course I made my share of mistakes, but you have to use your mistakes to learn and discover your potential. I found mentors wherever I could and truly listened to their counsel and observed their leadership methods.

I was fortunate to have my dad to look up to, because he was one of the best. He had all the values and quality of character that he had learned from his father, and he thoughtfully shared them with me. His discipline was firm and by the rules. Honesty, integrity, and applying the Golden Rule as a method of dealing with people were paramount to him. My grandfather, E.J., was soft-spoken, yet firm, and only had to tell you once to do something before you got moving. At times, people think being loud is strong and being soft is weak, but actually, the opposite may be true. Being quiet, you can show intelligence more convincingly than by talking, because the more you talk, the less believable and less intelligent you come across. E.J. was the epitome of using gentle, sound reasoning. He was a small man in stature who carried a big stick for what was right.

When my grandfather passed away, my dad moved into the leadership role with his brother as his partner. His brother George was half owner of the company, leading the golf wearables and golf ball sales divisions, while Dad managed the other divisions of the company. For years, George's time was mostly involved with the golf cart business, which he and my dad shared ownership. They later sold the golf cart business, and my uncle came back full time to the family company.

Our primary product distribution agreement was written with individuals who owned the company, not in the company name. In 1984, somewhat unexpectedly, that vendor wanted a change in our company's leadership and ownership structure. They were unhappy with the leadership on one side of our family business and cancelled the existing distribution agreement, which included all family members. They then awarded the distribution rights for their products to Wayne Smith Sr.'s side of the family. This included my dad, my brother Steve, and me. On the other side was my uncle and his son. This change split the company into two companies, and generated a complete reorganization. I was forty-four years old with a wife and two daughters. During that time, my dad was sick and in and out of the hospital, and his work time was limited. I quickly went from being a sales manager to being the CEO of a fifty-nine-year-old company, right in the beginning of a complete company restructure.

A few months after beginning the split, my Uncle George and his son initiated a lawsuit against us for "stealing" the company from them. It was a false claim, and they knew it, but they were hoping a jury would believe them. The discovery period lasted for three years with their lawyer trying to make it as difficult as possible for us at a time when we were under the stress of establishing a new company. I spent many nights during the three years uptown in the office of our attorneys going over every possible detail of the suit. Often, we were there until midnight. I gained a lot of respect for trial attorneys. The trial lasted for seven days. The opposing side produced only one witness (George's secretary) during the entire seven-day trial. We produced so many witnesses the judge asked us not to bring any more to the stand. The jury was out for only one hour deliberating and decided in our favor. The judge ordered they pay $130,000 for bringing a frivolous lawsuit.

We took fifty-eight people from the previous company's structure. The agreement called for us to move out of the current facility. During the initial months of the split, we agreed to share the existing building until our new headquarters was completed.

We had no building, no cars, no trucks, no IT systems, no operating software, no banking relationships, no legal relationships, and not enough people.

I was working on the design and construction of two new buildings for our company—one 100,000 square feet and the other 10,000 square feet. As the buildings went up, I constantly made design changes and additions to improve the functionality around our requirements. As it goes in construction, the change orders added to the cost and time. I had more on my plate than seemed possible to handle, and for years, I took no vacations.

We built on property down the street that we owned and encountered numerous issues with preparing the land for construction. I ended up getting an on-the-job education in building construction from the contractor. It was a time-consuming effort, on top of an already-full load of restructuring our corporation. I was interviewing and hiring new people as we took on the incredibly large task of transferring all appropriate data from the previous company to our company's processes with very little cooperation from our previous partners. The reorg included purchasing trucks and cars, designing a company logo, legal requirements for the new organization, acquiring and implementing new workflow procedures, restructuring vendor agreements, establishing a banking relationship, payroll procedures, structuring company operations, transferring customer relationships, and what seemed like never-ending tasks to be done.

The entire process was not something I ever expected to take on, but I sure learned a lot, from land planning to construction, IT, workflow, payroll management, vendor contracts, banking, legal, and HR—more than I imagined. I knew that if we were going to be as successful as I hoped, we were going to need the best people. Any organization setting high goals and expectations will need to start the journey with the right and engaged people. We were fortunate to bring fifty-eight of them with us who were in the two divisions we were assuming. We fully understood the job ahead was to fill our staff with the best people on the team.

*Any organization setting high goals and expectations will need to start the journey with the right and engaged people.*

I didn't think things could get much more difficult, but they did when I started having chest pains. I went to the ER on a few occasions, and each time they would tell me it was stress, not a heart attack. But it sure felt like a heart attack. That stress was something I had to internalize, because people do not want to see their leader under stress or with a lack of confidence. Hiding the stress issue was probably not the best way to deal with it, but I understood that the reorganization stage was not going to last forever, and I just needed to tough it out. Fortunately, after three years, things were finally in place and performing very well, and the pains ended.

We had a tremendous amount of confidence in our people, with their experience, talents, and their faith in the company direction and the opportunity before us. Everyone was taking pride in their contribution to our plan. They were excited about our accomplishments and for the future. This required a lot of hard work by all, but it was satisfying and fun as well.

The two divisions that we acquired in the company's split represented $10 million in gross revenue. At the time, we had two locations: the headquarters in Charlotte and a branch office in Hilton Head, South Carolina. When our chief financial officer (CFO) and I were visiting banks to establish a relationship, one of the bank vice presidents asked me what revenue we were going to be able to generate in our first year of operation. I told him $12 million. He replied that probably was not a realistic number, given that we were in a reorganization, and the bank would need a good number. I replied, "That is a good number." With our new customer- and product-focused approach and the experience and abilities of our people, I was very confident about our success. Well, we did not do $12 million that first year, we did $14 million! So, perhaps, in one sense, he might have been right. From two locations in two states, now we have twenty-one locations in four states, and are anticipating additions.

Early on, I brought our people together and asked them what we were going to be.

"We are going to be good," they said.

"How good?" I asked.

"The best in our territory," they said.

I replied, "Better than our competitor?"

They said yes.

"Is that it?" I asked.

"No, we are going to be the best distributor in the country."

"If we are going to be the best, how are we going to do that?"

"We are going to outwork our competition."

"Is that enough?"

"No, we are going to take care of our customers better than anybody."

"Now you've got it," I said. "We are going to be the best because of hard work and by taking care of our customers better than anyone else does—let's do it."

The building was completed, and we moved into a wonderful new facility with the changes needed to fit our business. We had an attached warehouse with increased storage and workflow layout designed for our products. A 10,000-SF service facility, a two-story office with meeting rooms, and specific workspaces for each department. We established a relationship with the bank (a new one, not the one that doubted my forecast), our operational software was in place and working, and our revenues were strong. I knew financials, but I did not know computers and software, so I took a day course at a local college so I could better understand IT. That probably was just enough to make me dangerous! With the help of some outside consultants, and a good IT manager, I learned enough to make things work.

Human resources, however, was somewhat of a challenge. I wrote a company handbook and was hiring people, but HR is far more than that. Neither my assistant nor I knew enough about all the legal regulations for correctly managing HR. Both of us became stressed about the volume of HR work we had on top of our already-full schedule, and eventually she resigned because I continued to overload her work capacity. That was a learning experience for me. When you have someone very talented who can accomplish almost everything, it is easy to overload them. That is exactly the mistake I made. I finally did the needed thing and hired an HR manager.

The reorganization had given us a new start with great people, and we now had the structure and ability to focus on the business's two product divisions—turf equipment and irrigation products. Now we were able to do things we could not have done as part of the previous company when we had limited resources stretched over five divisions and a constant play for money between divisions. Given the opportunity to restructure, focus, and expand capabilities, we were able to do many more things to make the company successful.

In 1987, our second full year of restructured operation, we won the National Distributor of the Year Award from The Toro Company. This was a great tribute to our people, to our new capabilities, and to our customer-centered focus. Our growth continued at a rapid pace through the 1990s, adding high-quality people, more locations, and new product lines. In 1992, we were asked to take additional territory responsibilities, adding most of Tennessee and thus expanding our operations to three states. In 2000 we purchased the Virginia distributor.

# Preface

During the 1990s, we were in a fast-paced growth environment in our industry. I didn't need to think very hard to understand that we either needed to make the investments and efforts to move with the industry or get out of the way. That brought opportunity, challenges, and new experiences for the entire team.

If you are open to it, learning really never stops throughout your entire career, and I was definitely open to the learning opportunities—on-the-job and otherwise—that came my way. That was all extremely helpful; but in reality, I think I learned and used a great deal of what I witnessed and learned from my dad and grandfather. Their influence on the business is still there today. Education and experience are great teachers, maybe the best. But for me, having good mentors was invaluable. There is much to learn listening to others who have a treasure trove of experience to share.

*If you are open to it, learning really never stops throughout your entire career.*

The business, now almost one hundred years old, is now under the leadership of the fourth generation. My daughter is president.

*Smith Turf & Irrigation Headquarters in Charlotte, North Carolina. STI has over 280 employees supporting and servicing customers in four states.*

*Over the years, STI has provided industry-leading product offerings for golf course maintenance and irrigation equipment.*

*STI has been a top distributor for Toro Golf Course Equipment for nearly one hundred years.*

*We know you...*

*STI is committed to their customers' success.*

# STI | SMITH TURF & IRRIGATION
### 1925   www.smithturf.com

*Pictured here is a portrait of E.J. Smith, Wayne B. Smith Sr., and Wayne B. Smith Jr.*
*E.J. Smith and Sons, today Smith Turf & Irrigation, was founded in 1925*
*on four basic principles: integrity, innovative products, exceptional service,*
*and an absolute commitment to the customer's success. Those four elements*
*became the benchmarks of the company and form the foundation upon which*
*Smith Turf & Irrigation was built.*

# ABOUT THIS BOOK

From sales representative to sales manager to CEO, I was able to develop many of my own thoughts and beliefs about leadership and business. I kept notes to myself that are the foundation for this book. If it was important, or something I needed to remember, I wrote it down. More than sixty years in business activities in different situations and environments have given me much happiness and satisfaction, but a few regrets too. My experience was at times challenging, sometimes stressful, but also rewarding, fun, and certainly worth the ride. I also had the opportunity to be involved in leadership roles outside the business world in a number of areas, including community, civic, sports, church, and charity. All have been great experiences that have allowed me to make valued acquaintances and friends. I consider myself fortunate to have had those opportunities and experiences.

Over my career, *in learning groups as well as at work,* I have been asked about my thoughts and beliefs on business issues. These have been great opportunities to share and to learn with other leaders and friends, and I am certain I learned more than I shared. One day I was visiting my attorney when once again business issues entered the discussion. She said, "You should write a book."

I had heard that before, and my standard answer was, "I am neither an expert, nor a writer, I just know what I believe. Also, I cannot type as fast as I can think."

She replied, "All you need is a dictation app, and then just start talking."

That is precisely what I've done: I downloaded an app and talked. I talked just as if you and I were sitting across the table with a cup of coffee. I actually believed I could talk through the four subjects in a week. That turned out to be not true. To talk through the subjects with thoughtful input took a significant amount of time.

There are four subjects in this book: Leadership, Culture, People, and Selling, and a very brief comment on Technology. The sections that follow are my concise discussions on those topics. I am not addressing current leadership methods of the newer generations of people, but rather tried and proven skills and principles that have endured and will endure the passage of time. These are basic approaches every leader and organization can use and rely on.

There is a steep learning curve in business, and if you pursue learning, a vast amount of information and opportunities are available. There are hundreds of very good books available to you on each of the topics I'm addressing. I knew I had a lot to learn, so I took the time and made the effort to acquire as much knowledge as I could. However, learning helps only if you use it. Recently, I read an excellent description: "Learning is the pursuit of what you don't know." You already know a lot—it is what you don't know that you learn. Having said that, you probably know, or should know, most of what I talk about. I am not revealing the unknown, I am addressing the known with what I think, learned, believe, and have used. I hope there are some graspable ideas and tenets included that you will utilize moving forward. This is not a playbook because there is no perfect playbook, as business issues are circumstantial, adaptive, and not always the same. Rather, this is a collection of ideas and principles you can use if they fit.

# Part One
# Leadership

# Chapter 1

## What is a Leader?

*The buck starts here—and the buck ends here.*

Every organization, team, committee, and group needs a leader. My grandfather and my dad both had strong character and great strength of will. They were successful leaders who were greatly admired by many. People used to say they would run through a brick wall for my dad. My grandfather, who survived going broke twice, was written about in a book titled *Men of Achievement in the Carolinas* by Leonard Johnson and Lloyd Smith. A person in our industry who did a lot of work with my dad used to punch me on the chest and say, "You'll never be half the man your father was." My answer was, "I'll take half," because that would still be very good.

Are leaders born or made? This is often discussed, and the answers are based on differing beliefs. Most people would say that leaders are made, and a survey suggests that 30 percent is genetic and 70 percent is learned. However, we have all seen very young people who step up and lead—captains of high school and college teams, chairpersons of volunteer organizations, you name it—where for them, leading organizations and people seems to be in their DNA. This leadership propensity follows them throughout their life, which is why I think a significant aspect of leadership is born in some people.

In my case, I had a desire to lead starting in the fifth grade when I was elected an officer of the school safety patrol. I knew then that I liked being in charge and making the decisions. Although the desire to lead was there from that young age, it was not fully engaged until much later. I seemed to be full of ideas, but not yet in a place to execute any of them, which was probably a good thing. When I did get into a leadership role, it fostered the desire, as well as the need, to learn as much as possible about how to be a good leader.

I was so fortunate to have my dad as a mentor. He trusted me enough to put me in significant roles and also to give me guidance and discipline when he believed it necessary. Early on, I made some leadership mistakes and took some liberties I should not have taken with a leadership status, both as a sales manager and later as CEO. This was nothing bad, I was just behaving as if I was still a team member, not a leader. I still wanted to be "one of the boys." I soon realized, however, that now that I was a leader, all eyes were on me. It was learn or fail, and I was not going to let my dad down by failing. I was very aware of the need to fill my dad's and granddad's shoes, and boy, those were big shoes to fill.

To succeed a great leader, no matter the endeavor, adds a unique challenge to the task. I knew that in order to be successful I would need to be intentional about learning all that I could. Leaders, whether born or made, develop over time, and there are not many shortcuts along the way to become successful. Theoretically, the more you do it, the better you should become.

*Leaders, whether born or made, develop over time, and there are not many shortcuts along the way to become successful.*

People can learn to be very good leaders through their education and experience. Even with those, having good mentors plays an essential role in the learning curve of a high-quality leader. I was lucky to have some good mentors in addition to my grandfather and dad. We all need people we can look up to and emulate. Even Abraham Lincoln had mentors, two of whom were Andrew Jackson and Henry Clay, both political rivals of his. Jackson and Clay challenged President Lincoln's thinking with other viewpoints, and that helped him with the decisions he needed to make. Lincoln was smart enough, or certainly wise enough, to seek counsel from others, even though they often held views different from his, as described in the book *Team of Rivals* by Doris Kearns Goodwin. From them and other notables like Zachary Taylor, Lincoln learned the valuable lessons of politics. Most all professionals—regardless if they are in sports, business, politics, or other areas—have trusted mentors whom they listen to and learn from. And these are not one-time lessons— the coaching and learning never stops. This is not to say you have to agree with every piece of advice they share, because ultimately, it is your responsibility to understand what you can learn and use.

There is no limit to the number of mentors you can learn from and emulate. Often you don't even need to go looking for them, they can appear fortuitously, even without a search. My friend Dr. Jerry McGee, former president of Wingate University, wrote about the mentors he had in his life in a book he gave to his children. In the book were twenty mentors. Jerry told me the mentors who helped him the most were the ones who demanded the most from him.

When I was a sales representative, our sales manager was a person everyone called "Big Daddy," both because of his physical size and the respect he received from everyone. He would call me into his office and start with: "Son, let me tell you something." He was wise in his unique way, and I learned so much from him. If you are open to it, you learn from people who aren't there to be nice to you, necessarily. You can learn immeasurably from others whose strengths you respect.

If you think back to your parents, teachers, coaches, and other key people in your life, you can see the wisdom in McGee's statement about learning the most from the demanding mentors who pushed him to excel. The perseverance people must demonstrate on their path to becoming a good leader is critical, because leadership is a never-ending journey. Things change, and consistent learning keeps you in the game. No matter your age or circumstances, there is always something to learn and places, opportunities, and people to learn from. You need to be wise enough, and perhaps humble enough, to recognize learning opportunities when they present themselves. Good leaders understand the benefits of learning from others and

*Good leaders understand the benefits of learning from others and take full advantage of opportunities for self-improvement.*

take full advantage of opportunities for self-improvement. Watch, listen, learn, and grow wise.

A leader is responsible for growth of the organization, for setting its direction, for the long-term vision of the organization, for positive influence, making critical strategic decisions, and taking the necessary risk for success. Leadership is not about status. It is about responsibility.

---

*A leader is responsible for growth of the organization, for setting its direction, for the long-term vision of the organization, for positive influence, making critical strategic decisions, and taking the necessary risk for success. Leadership is not about status. It is about responsibility.*

---

# CHAPTER 2

## LEADERSHIP QUALITIES

*What it takes to be a leader.*

While much has been written about the attributes a leader must have, leadership is not, and never has been, an exact science. It's about being adaptive, confident, humble, trusting, and accepting, and it's about solving challenges.

Universities can turn out smart, data-driven individuals who can transform a business, but those abilities alone do not make a successful leader. Why is there a difference between smarts and wisdom? Let's talk about the latest research from the University of California at San Diego on the human brain. It says the difference between intelligence and wisdom comes primarily from experiences. In order to attain the benefit of the experiences, one must be open-minded, compassionate, emotionally stable, and self-aware. Intelligence provides the answer to the question; wisdom provides the understanding of the question.

In addition, the research indicates some amount of wisdom could come from inheritance.

A great deal goes into a being a truly good leader, so let's talk here about some of those qualities that I believe to be paramount.

First, those who are in a leadership role should deserve the role they play. That requires the leader to have all the skills to do the job. John Maxwell wrote a book, *Developing the Leader Within You*, about the twenty-one qualities of leadership. His book is very good, and I am not attempting to create another list of leadership qualities. On most any topic, the top ten on the list are generally similar in content.

## Character

Character must be on every list of qualities a leader must have. Not only that, it should be number one.

To a certain extent, good character is something a person demonstrates in their life decisions. Those choices, decisions, how you think, and how you behave, in any number of situations and in all aspects of your life, determine the type of person you become. If you have made good ethical choices, you will have built the right character, the inner character, which will serve you well for life. It also entails learning from bad choices and not repeating them. Those life decisions often pit opposites against each other, such as emotional decisions, honesty decisions, win-lose, and involvement or no involvement choices, making it difficult to come to a decision. Having to choose between two options may mean that one will impact your life more than the other. One could benefit you more, but may not be the ethical decision to make. So those choices are what you decide to do or not to do. An athlete may want to go party the night before a game, but chooses not to. In a significant number of life choices, the opposing options could have one choice that means more in terms of consequences than the other. All choices have impacts, and thinking them through helps to make better decisions.

Character provides one with the ability to use self-control, a skill that any good leader uses every day in their leadership role. The leader's character can, and should, carry over to the organization as a whole and be an influence on its culture. I don't think you can be a good and successful leader if you are not first a person of good character. People say that dogs look like their owners, and I think that organizations look like their leader. This happens because organizations tend to take on the style, manner, behavior, and ways exhibited by their leader. If the leader exhibits a high level of integrity, the organization will likely reflect that same behavior. If a coach is competitive and emotional, the team will follow his intensity. Leaders, by their actions, show people not only how to get better, but how to be better. Leaders role model character.

Being a person of good character means you are ethical, have integrity, possess humility, are inspirational, open-minded, trustworthy, understanding, and confident. Leaders are culturally aware of their own beliefs and values, and they respect the different cultures of those they work with.

My grandfather was a great example of a man with good character. He did not curse, drink, or smoke. He conducted business not so much with contracts, but on his word, which was as good as any paper document. Once, when he hired a new sales representative, Jim, he told Jim to go call on a customer who was located about one hundred miles from the office. He gave Jim the price of the equipment and sent him on his way. When Jim returned with a check from the customer for the product, he told my grandfather he got more than the given price for the product. My grandfather told Jim to go back to the customer, return the check, and get a check for the amount he had stated, because the amount given was fair for the company and fair for the customer. That kind of fairness and integrity was how he conducted both the business and his personal life.

Imagine if that integrity were ingrained in leaders today.

## Competence

Competence is also a must, and number two on my list.

Leadership competence is not only what makes the organization's strategy succeed, but also overflows to instill confidence in its people. The objective is to have both good character and competence, but you cannot trade character for capability—or for anything else, in my opinion. There are those whose competence is exemplary, but they are just not good, or successful, leaders. There are others in a leadership position who clearly lack the character necessary to be in a leadership role. It takes a high degree of character to be a good leader—you simply need to be a good person to be good at leadership. The ultimate authority to lead is determined by the people who are led. They are intuitive enough to understand competence and character when they see it. Organizations historically use a competence-based approach to determine their leadership role, because competency combined with other skills creates leaders.

A whole set of skills define competency in a leader: the ability to envision beyond the obvious, the technique to communicate well, the skill to coordinate, intelligence, being influential, and being innovative. These all can determine your success in leadership. But you still have to have the right character to pull it off.

If you are at the intersection of character and capabilities, you are standing at a good place. Where these two things cross is where leadership resides. That intersection means you have to have the morals to do the right thing and the ability to do the right thing well—no matter what the situation dictates.

## Education

Education is at the core of leadership.

The importance of learning the skills of a leader is well understood. A master's degree in business administration (MBA) teaches management, organization structure, leadership foundations, financial principles, data utilization, planning, business principles, functions, and a great deal more.

A higher degree of learning will enhance earning potential, marketability, and career opportunities. It gives you opportunities to show and use learned skills. Education, and particularly business education, provides the skills and knowledge of the "how to" of managing a company successfully. Education is valuable and provides skills which are transferable to other endeavors for a lifetime.

I still believe that education will not make one a successful leader without the other abilities of leadership. A recent survey determined that CEOs are in the sixty-sixth percentile of IQ. That clearly revealed other qualities are very important in achieving leadership success. As valuable as a master's degree is, it is not an absolute. There are many individuals without an MBA who become outstanding leaders through their experience and learning opportunities. In addition to education, leaders of organizations retain things like people skills, charisma, and curiosity. Leaders are curious people in nature. To satisfy that curiosity they ask a lot of questions like Why? How? What? and even What do you think?—which I will talk about later. Regardless of how they attain it, a leader needs education to have the fundamentals of leadership, no matter the organization being led.

## Humility

Humble leaders practice emotional intelligence and appreciation for others.

My dad was a big believer in humility as a very important personal trait and leadership skill. He was the perfect example of that, as was my grandfather. Dad often gave people a piece of writing he'd found in a book that described the importance of and gains associated with humility when he thought someone would benefit from reading the message. He had a concern about people who became overconfident or cocky to the extent where it hurt both their personal relationships and leadership abilities. Sometimes overconfident people have a way of overestimating their abilities and underestimating everyone else's.

Humility is not a sign of weakness; it can be a source of strength—a point not enough people comprehend. It is the tempered confidence you have in yourself and your abilities to accomplish your objectives and to establish and maintain relationships. Your relationships and communications, as well as your business and personal decisions, are directly influenced by a certain degree of humility.

> ◈
>
> *Humility is not a sign of weakness; it can be a source of strength.*

# Leadership Qualities

Leaders are aggressive, hard-working, and confident for sure, but the best ones also have a sense of humility and know their own limits and strengths. Humility is about not being the center of things, but about the quiet ego of confidence. A sense of humility gives leaders the confidence to trust others and lead them effectively. It creates connections with people that overconfidence cannot achieve. Good self-awareness in leadership is about not letting an overblown ego take over. It is not about you—it is about the responsibility you accepted in becoming the leader. Sensitivity to others is part of the unique responsibility of being a leader, a parent, a friend, or mentor.

We have all seen leaders who were overconfident to the point of, "I am right, you are wrong, and let me tell you why." Unfortunately, those individuals simply do not have a good understanding of themselves, their place, their responsibilities, and do not think there is a chance they may be wrong. Theirs is the only opinion that matters. For many, it is difficult for them to let go of the need to be right. I found it difficult to effectively communicate with someone who took that type of approach; it sometimes gave me the feeling that it wasn't even worth trying. The "I'm right, you're wrong" people have no room for learning or improvement. They lack self-awareness—not where a leader should be if they want to be successful.

Humility allows you to understand that you are not always right, and that understanding is part of knowing who you are. A leader with good self-perception should always seek the truth and look for ways to improve themselves. As my dad told me, "Humility goes a long way toward getting you where you want to be as a person and as a leader of people." There is a balancing act between humility and having the confidence to lead that good leaders must master. You have to have the ability to get on a person's level if you want to influence and lead them, and you can't get there by thinking too much of yourself. A good question would be, "Would I follow me?" If the answer is no, or I'm not sure, then you would, in all probability, be better served choosing a non-leadership role.

## Courage

Along with confidence, it takes courage to lead.

There are enormous responsibilities that come with leading, from ensuring the financial success of the organization to resolving organizational issues. Performance failure is not an option in the job description of a leader. Often there are significant risks involved, and courage is needed to address difficult issues arising in challenging times. Fortunately, those are not an everyday occurrence, but when challenges present themselves, there is no "easy" button on the desk. The weight on the leader's shoulders is heavy, and it takes courage to move beyond your comfort zone and to rise up to meet the hard issues. During those tough times, you may need to call a time-out, have a team meeting with yourself, and reassure yourself by saying, "I can do this."

People will come to you about many issues when you are the leader. To them, you are expected to have all the answers, and sometimes you just don't. If you don't have the answer, by all means say so. You need to have the honesty and courage to say, "I don't know." Bluffing your way through it will only cause bigger problems later, because the bluff will show itself, and you will have lost creditability. If a person comes to you with a need-to-know-now question, you need to find the answer in as timely a manner as possible, or you will begin to lose favor as a trusted resource. Timely, knowledgeable responses are what people expect from any leader. Therefore, a clear understanding of the reasonable timeline for a response should be established up front to alleviate any frustrations that may develop from possible delayed answers. People will equate late, or unmade, responses with a lack of motivation, responsibility, or even creditability. As a leader, you certainly do not have to be the smartest person in the room. But you need to possess the overall attributes necessary to be the leader.

## Self-Awareness

Good and great leaders are very much in tune with themselves.

Many people begin with certain innate skills, which will be their basic strengths throughout life, and thus will help shape them into who they will later become. Good leaders have the confidence to know who they are, as well as the confidence to know who they are not. In order to be successful, people must understand their strengths and weaknesses. They must know how to make their unique combination of skills work for them in a positive and successful manner. Moreover, they should be willing to change or improve in both personal and professional areas.

"Know thyself," said the ancient philosopher Socrates.

They must check in with these questions: Who am I? What am I good at? What am I not so good at, and how will I improve? Who do I want to be, and who do I not want to be?

Leaders, as well as others who "get it" about themselves, are more successful in their careers and have better personal satisfaction in life. Self-awareness embodies our perception and understanding of ourselves, as well as our personal aspirations and long-term goals. While personality tests can be a helpful aid in learning about ourselves, much of this understanding comes from our everyday life experiences and our interactions with our parents, family, faith, teachers, friends, and people we respect. Think about the content and manner of your communication, your emotions, and your behavior and what they tell you about yourself. All good contributors to your understanding of just who you are.

While self-awareness is primarily an internal consideration, it helps to have an understanding of others' perceptions of us. Often a 360-degree evaluation (and other tools like it) conducted by your peers and reports will reveal the self-truth that a good leader needs to know. One needs to accept the outcomes of these kinds of evaluations in a positive manner in order to derive benefits from their findings. If you don't understand your weaknesses and flaws as well as you understand your strengths, then you do not have good self-awareness.

*If you don't understand your weaknesses and flaws as well as you understand your strengths, then you do not have good self-awareness.*

Being defensive about your efforts, decisions, or beliefs can short-circuit the results of any self-awareness improvements, no matter the source of the information. If you tend to be on the defensive side, then that is definitely something you need to understand about yourself and work to correct. Being defensive drives people away from communicating with you in a meaningful way. People learn that whatever they say will have an opposing rebuttal and thus no effective communication, or any understanding, will happen. Soon they will be unwilling to communicate with you at all. If you are overly defensive, much of the value in the forthcoming information will be diminished, if not lost altogether.

# Leadership Qualities

A friend of mine, a business owner, used one of these 360-degree evaluations to improve communication and interactions with a new partner in his company with whom he was having relationship difficulties. The resulting personal understandings worked very well for both of them, as they learned how to communicate with each other more effectively. One was a "just-the-facts" person who wanted a straight delivery and no extras, while the other was a storyteller who might take a while to get to those facts. Each of them became willing to make changes so that things would work better between them.

There is a good book, *Soar with Your Strengths*, by Donald Clifton and Paula Nelson, which speaks to self-awareness and the ability to use your strengths to help you become successful. Learn your strengths and use them, and they will be stronger than your weakness. If you are going to use your strengths, you need to know what exactly they are. Perhaps you need to pause and think about what you do well and what you enjoy doing. Good things happen when you are doing what you enjoy. Stress happens when you do things you do not enjoy. Pursue the things you enjoy doing, both personal and professional, and to the best extent possible, exclude things that cause stress and unhappiness.

---

*Good things happen when you are doing what you enjoy.*
*Stress happens when you do things you do not enjoy. Pursue the things*
*you enjoy doing, both personal and professional, and to the best*
*extent possible, exclude things that cause stress and unhappiness.*

---

The other side of the coin is knowing what your weaknesses are. If you understand your weakness, you can work to improve it, or simply stop doing it. If you do not enjoy being a leader, with all the associated responsibilities and characteristics, then you should probably not choose leadership. You could be a wonderful person who has no interest in managing others, and that's okay!

Take a look at the qualities you either have or do not have, because they can determine how successful you are as a leader. Honesty, integrity, caring, morality, and other attributes are not qualities that you can turn on only when needed. If someone turns on and off those qualities, then he or she is simply faking and using those attributes when necessary for a purpose, and really does not possess them. Good personal qualities are yours all the time; they are not part-time characteristics. Professionally, this becomes so important because organizations take on and emulate the behavior, character, and style of the leader. People emulate what they see: monkey see, monkey do. If someone sees quickly through any exhibited pretense, they will categorize you as a fake. Any leader lacking the attributes of good character will not be the leader the organization will need and will not have a successful following.

Individuals who become leaders can learn much about leadership through their education, experiences, and their innate skills. Predominantly, leaders have good intellectual abilities, and many have deep educations in their repertoire. However, all the education one can get will not be enough to enable you to become a good leader if the other important leadership characteristics—communication, self-awareness, integrity, character, passion, and vision—are not there. Smarts alone simply will not make someone a good leader. Sometimes even smart people do not see the issues, which are critical to success. While knowledge should lead to wisdom, often it just does not, as self-awareness and strong character are far more useful than book knowledge.

Additionally, good leaders should also have a certain amount of street smarts, or common sense. Street smarts, or intuition, can help you handle any situation that may arise by paying attention to what's going on around you and making safe decisions based on common sense solutions. Both Dad and Granddad had a degree of street smarts, which allowed them to make business decisions around the customer's desires and to help counsel employees at all levels.

## Experience

Experience is a process of learning by doing.

Experience is a great teacher; many argue it is the best one. Every experience contributes valuable building blocks for making you who you are and determining how successful your leadership will be to an organization. The more experience you have, the more you learn, and the better you become. So much is gained by experience, and experience matures over time. You get to wear the "been there done that" T-shirt. Innate talent, learning, and experience, in combination with other personal attributes, develop the best leaders. No matter the occupation, experience largely comes from doing the job, not from education, and one needs to seek out as many opportunities as possible because the wider your range of experience, the more things you will learn.

Actually doing a job, or many jobs, is on-the-job training. Experience means doing, and it provides discovery, reflection, and a significant amount of self-education. If you do something yourself, your knowledge retention, thinking, and beliefs about the process is improved. You retain the facts. You learn more and understand the concept quicker because it is purpose-driven training. This is exactly why my dad moved me from job to job around the company. I confess that I did not totally understand his purpose for doing this at the time. Theoretically, the more diversity in your on-the-job experience, the better your skills become.

## Time Management
It is the intelligent use of your time.

Time management, or the effective use of one's skills, should be prevalent, no matter your role, professional or personal. This is an important personal attribute for everyone, and it increases in importance when you are a leader. Being the leader does not give you the right or permission to be untimely in any part of your responsibilities. It does not matter if your communication is verbal, written, in person, or anything else; you must be consistently on time, all the time. Timeliness is particularly important for meetings and appointments requiring your attendance. In the minds of the attendees, as the leader, you do not have their approval to stroll in late, sending to all the message that you and your time are more important than they are. That is a strong message of disrespect to people, and believe me, they will not forget it. There is no "socially late" protocol permissible in any activity where you are responsible for being on time. If anything, the leader should be the first one present. I tell my daughters that starting times in golf are not approximate, and neither is anything else where you have a designated time to be present—period. Constant tardiness results in a significant loss of credibility and confidence from others. It will inexorably affect your ability to lead people successfully. I have witnessed consistent tardiness put a strain on personal relationships between friends and the relationship end because of the persistent lateness of a person or persons. Professionalism is no different, and being late will result in a loss of respect. One of our VPs told a subordinate, "There is only one reason a person is late—you did not start on time."

A closed-door office routine is not good enough to enable a person to be effective as a leader. While leaders do need some time uninterrupted, they should not lose the benefits of interaction and awareness derived from exchanges with people and observations of happenings within the organization. A leader's closed-door practice can also create fear among their employees: i.e., "Don't interrupt—I'm too busy/important." You need to be aware of what is happening beyond the daily scope of your space. I say this because I have seen some (not many) business leaders who, for whatever reasons, were simply unaware of issues beyond their immediate purview or office door. It is easy to get caught up in your tasks and not make the effort to reach out and know what is transpiring elsewhere. A behavior which is not an effective use of time.

A good friend asked me to visit his company when I was visiting his city. When I entered the office and asked to see him, the receptionist said he was upstairs in his office and she would let him know I was there. While waiting for him, I talked to some people I knew who were in the downstairs office and learned that when John came in, he would go up to his office and rarely come out for the remainder of the day. The comment was, "He has no idea what goes on down here, he is just looking at the numbers." I really wanted to say something to John, but discretion took over and I did not bring it up. But it was a lesson learned for me to limit the time my office door was closed.

## Vision

Vision is the ability to think about the future with wisdom and imagination.

I served several years as a Chamber of Commerce Council Vice President, and I had the opportunity to attend a meeting presenting the next year's plan. The presentation was excellent and clearly shared the very positive vision of the upcoming year with the responsibilities inherent in achieving the plan, the roles we would each have for success, and finally, what the expected results of our efforts were going to be. Although my group was not a big part of the Chamber, I was glad to have been there to hear such a well-done presentation.

Leaders must have a good vision or direction and destination for the future of the organization. Vision ranks with trust and competence as one of the top qualities of a leader. A clear and compelling vision is the road map to guide the company's direction. While a leader cannot perfectly predict the future, they do need to know what is going to work in the future. When leaders are good at communicating their vision, it becomes the vision of the employees. People love knowing the vision and direction of the organization, and it generates positive attitudes associated with that shared knowledge. They feel and understand the value of their efforts in moving the organization forward. Not sharing and communicating a vision for the future leads to lower motivation among the staff, lower job satisfaction, and lower morale.

*Great leaders know where things stand in their company, the direction things should be going, and they set the expectations, realistic goals, standards, methods, and the process to get there.*
*The vision is free (thoughts)—the execution costs (money).*

# Leadership Qualities

Great leaders know where things stand in their company, the direction things should be going, and they set the expectations, realistic goals, standards, methods, and the process to get there. The vision is free (thoughts)—the execution costs (money). Leaders are the ones who climb the tallest tree, look around, and say, "We are going this way." The managers then make it work. This kind of forward thinking and vision will get people motivated and involved in the mission.

I enjoyed spending time thinking of all the possibilities for our company—What if . . . ? What can we be? Where are we going? How are we going to get there? What can we do better? Time spent on these big-picture issues is time well spent, but is often hard to come by because of your daily responsibilities. Leaders have to have the ability to see what is really out there (vision) in terms of opportunities and forward success, not just what is assumed to be out there. Keeping up with what is currently transpiring in the industry allows creditability into your elective thought process. Some visions come to life; some do not. But this kind of creative thinking is what leaders do and are expected to do.

Leaders develop the plans, chart the map, and share the vision. Oftentimes, issues cause visions to become obsolete before you can even implement them. When time is the dominant issue, it can be difficult for a vision to move at, or ahead of, changing conditions. Today's fast-paced competitive environment does not give you much time to sit around thinking about something, no matter its importance. Things you might have thought were long-term become more immediate. This means you must make the best decision you can make with the information you have now—not later. Vision must have timeliness in order for it to be successful, and it must be shared and transacted. Nothing happens till something happens; therefore, execution of the vision becomes the success factor.

Leaders know how to tap and use all the resources available to them in executing the vision. The best of the resources is talented people using their individual skills and capabilities to do the work necessary to achieve the desired results. You need buy-in from the people, and people need to understand their efforts are critical to the overall success of the company. To achieve that buy-in, you should share the vision openly, often, to make the move forward become a reality.

*You need buy-in from the people, and people need to understand their efforts are critical to the overall success of the company.*

Where do you get the vision? In a number of ways, actually. A significant amount comes from the experiences you have over time in both your business and personal life. You see how things are accomplished, or not accomplished, and why. You read and learn about success stories and failures. You communicate frequently with others, ask questions, and take in as much knowledge as possible. Some of your best thoughts and ideas can often come from "drive time thinking," or even at night when you are trying to sleep. You think innovatively, develop your ideas, and share them. Sometimes you have to think beyond what seems obvious or easily obtainable. Dream a little. Dreams are not only for sleeping!

My vision developed over time watching Dad and Granddad and from my six years of sales experience and many years of sales management. Plus the different civic work in which I had the opportunity to be involved gave me ideas as well. At the time of our reorganization,

I had over twenty years of experience. I watched our fellow distributors, as well as the competitors, and had a good idea of what worked and did not work for them. I saw opportunities there, as well as in our company that could improve performance. From the beginning of the reorg our objective was to be the best—"better than all the rest" as the song says. I knew we had great people who could execute the opportunities, given the chance to do so. Also, execution would involve the risk of front loading the investments to create the resources and capabilities needed to go to the next level. We implemented ideas, new practices, changes, and it worked. A trade publication described our company as "unmatched excellence." Great people, higher customer service and care, and other higher-level capabilities of which we were early adopters pushed us to the front. I am pleased to say that now most all others in our industry have made the steps to provide significantly better performance. A rising tide lifts all ships.

A note from one of our suppliers said, "One would have to be deaf, dumb, blind, and not too bright not to be impressed with what you have put together. . . . Your overall marketing strategy and commitment to professionalism and growth is unique among distributors in the industries that I have served or that have been affiliated with in my career." This note gave me enormous pride.

## Decisiveness

Decisiveness is a vital leadership skill.

It is critical that a leader has the ability, courage, willingness, and desire to make decisions. An inability to make decisions will most often determine if a person is capable of being a leader. If this skill is missing or not done well, leadership will in all probability fail. Procrastinating on making a decision is detrimental to any organization, no matter its size or scope. Not only can it result in missed opportunities and other failures, it also negatively affects the attitudes and work performance of the people. Procrastination is the opposite of action. Procrastination kills progress—period. It's like a habit-forming drug, and like a bad drug, it can have serious consequences. Some people are slow making decisions, and the more you allow that to be your method, the harder it becomes to break the habit. You can miss out on acquiring a new product line, hiring an outstanding candidate, and other consequential opportunities. Decisions of all descriptions are virtually a daily, if not hourly, responsibility of leading.

Planning fosters decisions. However, a plan is only a plan until it is activated. It can be on paper, on someone's mind, or in conversations, but until you actually put it to work, it remains a plan. It has been said a bad plan is better than no plan. Or as they say no decision is a decision, no plan becomes a plan. Neither of those are good. Without a plan, you're just hoping. Planning is creative thinking about using the resources you need to direct what you will do going forward. A plan is the actions, tasks, and timeline required to complete a goal. You have to be clear on what those next steps are, and with commitment and motivation, those steps change from "to do" to "done." Otherwise, it can become time wasted. Intentions, no matter how good they are, don't make things happen—actions do. If you intend to take your medications and do not take them, it will not be good for your

*A bad plan is better than no plan. Or as they say no decision is a decision, no plan becomes a plan.*

health. Plans require visions of the possibilities out there. It is what you want to achieve and turning ideas into reality, and it requires a significant number of considerations. When Howard Schultz bought Starbucks from his partners, he had a plan. Clearly, he did an outstanding job of turning his plan and vision to reality.

Decisions lingering longer than necessary become disruptive, demoralizing, and unfair to the people and the organization. We all know the phrase "paralysis by analysis"—very little positive comes from that kind of stalemate. There is a tipping point at which more analysis, or thinking about it, does not produce better results. A good plan executed is better than a delayed plan waiting for the perfect unexecuted plan. Not only could delayed decisions inhibit results, prolonging any needed decision also carries a real cost risk. Good leaders do not favor exhausting analysis over action because they possess a good understanding of when the time has come to stop thinking, make the decision, and act.

Leaders understand what the right information is in making decisions. Their experience facilitates their ability to separate the important from unimportant information and make good judgments. Sometimes it is the "been there, done that" factor. The objective is to think everything through, but often, as hard as you try, you can't think of every scenario. However, you cannot make decisions with weak information either. Making decisions is just something you get better at over time; the more you do it, the easier it becomes.

Frequently, circumstances dictate that you do not have time available to delay decisions. When time becomes the dominant factor, execution then is more important to success, and you just have to trust your intuition, as that can be a valuable tool in the process.

A leader cannot be afraid to make decisions because there might be some risk involved, as there seems to always be some amount of risk in any decision. Additionally, you cannot avoid making decisions just because you don't like to make decisions or are uncomfortable with the issue. Again: Most often, no decision is a decision—and often the wrong one. There is no question hard decisions are difficult to make, rendering them easy to avoid. Those could be terminations, cost reductions, new products, or other significant issues. Good leaders are good decision makers because they must be. They need to be able to successfully solve myriad challenges and issues in the ever-changing leadership role.

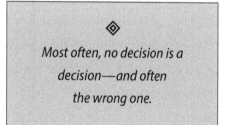

*Most often, no decision is a decision—and often the wrong one.*

I always tried to give our people an answer as soon as I could give it, preferably immediately after the request or question. I tried to say yes more than no because of the trust I had in the competence of our managers to know what they needed, and their responsibility to not ask for unnecessary resources. They knew the rules, and they knew asking for real needs was more likely to get a yes, and frivolous asks would likely get a no. There were times when I had to tell people who came to me for answers that they had not done their homework, and they needed to get that done first and then come back. I also liked to make an effort to indicate to them where the holes were in their plan, and then let them do it. Overall, our managers knew our business, and they understood what was needed and necessary for us to be successful. I trusted their input.

Years ago, a sales representative came to our office to show me a new product being introduced to the market. He invited me outside to demonstrate the product. Once there, he lifted this long shaft out of his vehicle. On one end, it had a very large two-cycle engine. On the other end of the shaft were nylon cords. He fired it up and went along the wall of our office cutting grass. He then handed it to me to try. It was big, heavy, and hard to hold.

After the demonstration, we went to my office and he asked, "What do you think about the product?"

I replied, "I don't think we want it, and here are the reasons. First, it is so heavy that it will be hard to use for very long. Second, the nylon cords will wear out very quickly, and will have to be replaced too often. You have to get better cords. Third, you need to change the name. 'Weed Eater' is the dumbest name I have ever heard for a product."

He left and went to our main competitor; they took on the product. They sold two truckloads before they even received their first shipment! Of course, neither he nor I knew the manufacturer would change to a smaller, lighter engine and upgrade those nylon cords and make more models. Fortunately, a few years later, Poulan, a line we did carry, bought Weed Eater and we ended up with the product. Obviously, nylon cord trimmers now come in many versions by several manufacturers and are sold in the hundreds of thousands. But I was the smart guy who turned down Weed Eater.

Not every decision you make will be a good one.

Admittedly, making a decision too quickly can also often lead to a wrong decision. The focus needs to be on making the best possible timely decisions, providing for successful outcomes. I also believe there are circumstances where correcting a wrong decision works better than dealing with the consequences of a delayed, or unmade, decision. Clearly, there are some situations that you cannot be 100 percent sure about, and that is where your experience and best judgment come into play.

One time, at a dinner function, my assigned seat was next to a nice young lady. During our conversation, she asked about where I worked and what my job was. I told her I was the CEO, to which she replied, "What does a CEO do?" Well, a definitive answer to that would have probably taken the remainder of the evening. I thought about it for a bit, and then said, "I make decisions." A very short, but true, answer. JeVon McCormick, in his book *Modern Leader*, confirms this as well. "Being a leader is largely about making decisions. As a leader . . . You're a decision engine."

This leads me to one of my favorite sayings: "Done is better than perfect." Or, as my wife likes to say, "Don't let perfect get in the way of good." Perfection is almost impossible, so seeking perfection in decisions is not only time-consuming, but can also be nonproductive.

*"Done is better than perfect." Or, as my wife likes to say, "Don't let perfect get in the way of good."*

If a leader is indecisive, inconsistent, untimely, or unresponsive, people will begin to wonder: Who is leading the organization—who is driving this bus? If it is not the designated leader, they begin to look elsewhere, and to other people, for needed answers. This can cause a loss of confidence in the leader, which will spread throughout the organization, and staff performance—and the organization's performance—will go down with it.

Indecisiveness and procrastination are kissing cousins. If one is not good at making decisions, they probably are also prone to procrastinating. If that is the case, then it will be a major problem for the person to be a good and effective leader for any organization.

I was more of a risk-taker than my dad, by far, and that included decisions. His conservative approach worked fine for the time he led the company; but times change, and his approach would probably fall behind in today's world. No doubt, I took more chances on what I and our managers saw as opportunities—new products, more locations, great people—to stay ahead of the game. Leadership challenges change over time, and leaders and leadership skills simply have to adapt and change with the moving environment.

## Passion

Passion is an intangible part of what makes some people leaders and others not.

Everyone has passion, right? Yes, to some degree, but great leaders seem to have a different level of passion. They have strong emotions and a higher level of caring about their endeavors. They bring determination and resiliency to the job of leading, every day, and that enthusiasm radiates throughout the organization and motivates others. They are passionate about the success of the organization, and the really good ones care about the success of their people. People pursue what they are passionate about, where their heart is, and work becomes enjoyable when they can achieve this in their lives.

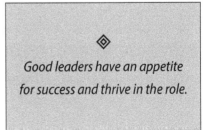

*Good leaders have an appetite for success and thrive in the role.*

Career becomes more than a job. Leaders have a strong belief in what they do and understand how this belief can contribute to the organization and motivate others. Good leaders have an appetite for success and thrive in the role.

Are they passionate about their personal success as well? Sure, everyone cares about his or her personal success. Leaders just seem to care more, with a high internal drive both professionally and personally. Leadership is not easy, and it is their persistent work habits that make the difference. They are driven by good results and using all of the methods to achieve those results. You can often see and feel the passion in a leader—it just shows. It is their drive to get things done, to make things happen, and for success. Passion and effort go hand in hand. The greater your effort, the greater your success. It is an internal professional and personal satisfaction that helps keep a leader's life in balance.

Passionate leaders are consistent in their pursuit for excellence, and they have a low tolerance for failure. That is not to say they do not allow some degree of failure by their people as a learning experience, because that is what good leaders do. Leading is so demanding, that if you simply do not have the passion it takes to lead, then leading is not

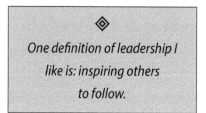

*One definition of leadership I like is: inspiring others to follow.*

for you, as it will likely do the opposite of keeping your life in balance. Passionate leaders are totally committed to achievement for the organization, their people, and themselves. Their passion is inspirational.

**Inspiring Others**

One definition of leadership I like is: inspiring others to follow.

I have always believed that a leader must constantly look over their shoulder and make sure people are following. People will not follow you if they don't believe in you and believe that you care about them, their success, and the success of the organization. They must believe in you before they will believe in your leadership. People truly follow a leader because they want to, not because they have to. They have other career options available to them.

People may actually like you as a person but will not follow you because of some failure in your leadership skills, character, methods, or habits. Your success as a leader—inspiring others and having people follow—will depend on earning both like and respect. Neither is a given—both are earned. Employees may give you the benefit of the doubt initially, but time will show whether you can earn both the like and respect. So, if a leader is inspiring, they motivate people to accomplish goals they may not have accomplished on their own. That leadership inspires others to be successful and contributes to good habits and attitudes. They inspire stimulating behavior in people and organizations.

**Trust**

Along with character, trust is the most important component of a leader's attributes.

Leaders spend a lot of time and effort on building trust in the organization, and with those in the organization. That is because trust starts from the top. How do you build that all-important trust with your people? You do it by first trusting them—by being able to relate to them, by building a team environment, and by getting them to work together. It must be a real and demonstrated trust, not a synthetic one. If a leader violates the trust between himself and his subordinates, the people will change what they think and believe about the leader. Unfortunately, there are many ways to breach the trust, from promises not kept, to saying one thing and doing another, to poor personal behavior. That is not something anyone wants to happen, and that is why I hold trust so highly. It takes concerted effort to not only build trust, but also to maintain it, because it is too important to be something you achieve and drop. Leaders need to be aware of everything they do in order not to damage or lose the trust of their people. You may think something you do or say is inconsequential, but it may not be to the people following you. You better believe they are watching and listening!

Baseball player Satchel Paige said, "Don't look back, something may be gaining on you." I like to change that a little by saying, "Look back to see if anyone is following you," because that is an indicator of your leadership effectiveness. Leaders must have the trust of their followers, because if they do not have trust in leadership, then work performance deteriorates. They may not be following you, and if they are not following, then your leadership is in trouble. Good leaders inspire others to trust and follow them, and therefore their loyalty is something that should be recognized. Done well will mean that people share the vision, feel valued, have job satisfaction, and demon-

---

*The interaction with your people—and the exchange of thoughts, ideas, and information—allows associates to see who you are, what you value, and the direction of the organization.*

---

strate teamwork. You see this in sports teams where the coach brings encouragement, excitement, and confidence to the team. Business is much the same, and leaders need to continually instill inspiration and confidence in their managers, as well as in their employees.

As a measure of your leadership's effectiveness, you need to check the temperature of your people frequently by making time to communicate with them. The interaction with your people—and the exchange of thoughts, ideas, and information—allows associates to see who you are, what you value, and the direction of the organization. Is your leadership style consistent? Are they energetically following? Do they trust you? Have they bought into your and the organization's plans? Stay in touch with the people, and be transparent in a good and positive way.

Trust is not just between leader and followers, it is present within the entire organization. Personal interactions are built on reliability, dependence, and trust between people. Consistent confidence in work relationships is dependent on mutual trust. A trust-orientated environment is enterprise-wide and deep, directly effecting the overall success.

All this is especially important when there is a change in leadership. New leaders need to earn the trust and respect of the people they are leading through their actions and the example they set. This trust-building needs to happen

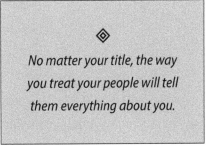

*No matter your title, the way you treat your people will tell them everything about you.*

right from the start of their leadership, or any changed role. Do not wait to exhibit the right example, because later may be too late. When I followed Dad and Granddad into leadership, I had a very high standard to follow, and absolutely had to have a good start. Their shoes were almost too big to fill, and even today, with over sixty years of experience, I still feel some of that challenge. When a leadership change occurs, you only get one chance to create a first impression, so do it right.

As a leader, people will judge you more by your actions than by what you say. An extension to the Golden Rule (which Dad used as a leadership principle) might be that no matter your title, the way you treat your people will tell them everything about you. This was one of the first lessons I learned. Leaders must walk the talk of what they want their people and the organization to be, because your reflection is what the organization will be. Dad said, "If you want to be the boss, you need to act like one." A car motor will not run properly if it is not "in tune"—and organizations will not function well if leadership and people are not "in tune." It becomes a disconnect between leadership and those led. Simply said: don't model the behavior you don't want to become or you don't want others to become, whether it is the business or even your personal life.

I was able to experience the building of trust, like, and respect for me during our company's reorganization. I was implementing a number of new changes, and initially a few people were unsure of the plans and therefore of me. They expressed their concerns with some of the new ideas, so I was very aware of what needed to occur to justify the impending changes and to gain their trust and support. During the transition, they were watching not only the success of new changes, but also me and my leadership skills. Being new in this leadership role, I was watching their reactions closely. A number of one-on-one conversations took place during the time, which kept me abreast of their feelings. I shared my vision with them, because they needed to know and understand where we were going and how we were going to get there. That included hiring additional people, implementing new processes, bringing on additional products, and building new facilities. I needed to share this information for them to have confidence in the plan and their efforts. I began to hear "we trust you," or "we are counting on you." The temperature was right, and they were enthused!

I decided to establish a call center. At the time, few, if any in our business had call centers. I knew if I could handle a customer's call from start to finish, other people could do it too. I called them together and announced the change. A few days later, one of the guys came into my office and said, "We have been talking and we don't think we can make the call center work, because each of us has specific product knowledge."

My reply was, "If I can do it, you can do it, and that is what we are going to do."

"How are we going to learn the other products?" he asked.

"We are going to teach you guys." Then I looked at him and said, "Are you in or out? Because if you do not want to be part of the center, you will be out, and I need your answer before you get out of that chair."

He was shocked and said, "We did not think you were that serious, but I am in."

I told him since he was the spokesperson to go back and relay the message to the group. It was a firm way of asking for trust. Once the new call center opened, it took only a couple of months for us to see how much our customers appreciated the ease of doing business with us. It was a tremendous success, and the team totally bought in to the concept.

The proof of good leadership is in the results that you, your people, and your

*Together we achieve more.*

organization achieve. It is like this: together we achieve more. Servant leadership is the opportunity to serve in many ways. Therefore, knowing the productive success of the people to the whole is something leaders closely watch along with the numbers. All measurements are important for determining what the organization's current success is and what future success will be. It is how to know if you are winning or losing. Success in any organization does not happen by accident; it is a total team effort. Setting high standards for work, focusing on those standards, and holding people accountable to the standards is what produces good results. Any ambiguity, deviation, or loss of efforts in the process will lead to some degree of stagnation and diminished performance.

## Taking Responsibility

Taking unconditional responsibility is of vital importance in establishing one's credibility as a leader.

A leader or manager not only holds himself or herself responsible, he or she also does not look for blame, even while holding others responsible. If there is a cause for blame, he or she takes the blame and does not attempt to avoid the responsibility. There is

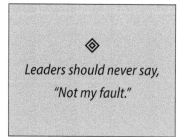

*Leaders should never say, "Not my fault."*

no passing the buck or playing victim in effective leadership. Leaders must be accountable in all aspects. This personal responsibility is the ability to act positively and effectively in relation to whatever events occur, because the right actions are what results depend on. Leaders who attempt to dodge personal responsibility will lose the trust of the people in the organization, and thus risk losing their role as leader. The better response is, "Thank you, that is a good point, I understand." Players do not want to go into the huddle after a fumbled play and hear the quarterback say, "Not my fault." Leaders step up to the challenge, take responsibility when required, and address the issue. All of which means leaders have to get comfortable with being held accountable, because it is a heavy load to carry.

## Influence

Being influential is about more than behavior, it is about setting people's mindsets to achieve a goal.

Influential leadership uses encouraging tactics to motivate people and organizations to achieve higher results. It is not based on power or control, and to be effective it relies on positive relationships because it drives change. Influence is not the same as inspiring people. They are similar, but different in purpose. Inspiring means uplifting and encouraging others, and has effect. Influence is primarily driving change. Being influential will affect change in something in an indirect way.

I began to notice as a leader that I could get things done in a more subtle manner by hinting or suggesting ideas in a conversation rather than giving a directive. Those suggested ideas would influence the person or persons to act on what I was thinking. Doing this allowed people to use their own skills in the process of making it happen, which, in a way, became their idea, not mine. In fact, when I asked them about it, they said "we" did this or that, and did not mention my name. I was talking to one of our sales managers about some specific use products, and I casually said it would be great if our customers knew we offered those as a group. A while later he came to me with a product brochure he put together with all of the like-kind products listed. He said, "I thought this would be a good thing to do." Right! You are trying to influence people to do the right things each day to make them successful. It did not always work, but it did enough times for me to see that I could influence people in different ways.

Leaders are influential people, and the ability to influence others plays an important part in their leadership responsibilities. The influence leaders have on people goes far beyond getting things done within an organization; it can change people's personal behavior as well. I watched my dad's fatherly approach to individuals, not only in the company but also to the many other people who looked up to him for his counsel. He counseled on personal problems, helped them solve issues when they were in trouble, and loaned money to help someone out of a problem. Like his dad, he gave sound advice to so many that I cannot even count the number of people who told me stories of his help and wisdom at times when they needed it the most. To some, they said his influence changed their life.

From business to sports to faith, leaders who are good role models influence others in their work ethic, personal behavior, and attitudes. The ability to positively influence others is not the same as coercion or directing. It is motivating individuals to achieve the common goals of the organization as well as life itself. Leaders and mentors use their influence to develop individuals and create a positive and cooperative environment in the organization. They influence others by setting the tone and the example for others to follow.

# CHAPTER 3

## TOOLS FOR LEADERSHIP

*The more tools you have in your toolbox, the better leader you will be.*

From serving your staff to delegating tasks, good leaders develop and use a number of tools to guide their leadership, support others, and help their organizations achieve goals.

### Servant Leadership

Servant leadership is a practice of leading by serving the people and the organization.

It is a great way to lead, and not easily achieved. To practice servant leadership, a leader needs to understand that it is not about him or her. It is about individuals for whom you are responsible and making them successful. It is having the humility to know your role as a servant who is leading and the ability to collaborate with talented colleagues in a supportive manner, allowing them to exercise their skills. Egos go away and he or she leads by example, giving people the opportunity to be successful.

To accomplish servant leadership, the leader needs to possess good self-awareness, focusing on the team's success rather than their own personal interest. As a servant leader, you are looking for ways and resources to help people do their job better without doing it for them. You are successful if the people are successful, and the organization is successful if the people are successful. Therefore when you expand your horizons to include people and help them be as good as they can be, you will increase the odds of your success.

Servant leadership brings out each individual's best abilities and makes use of these talents to benefit the organization. It generates personal fulfillment, job satisfaction, and work efficiency in the organization. Servant leaders spend time encouraging creativity in their people to help achieve the overall success generated in this environment. In order for servant leadership to work properly for people at all levels of the organization, people need to be respected and trusted to perform their job responsibilities. The leader understands he or she is there to serve others rather than be served: "I am here to help you be better and successful in your responsibilities." Inherent in servant leadership is that it is always "we," not "me."

Seeing people achieve success was one of the most rewarding parts of any job I had. To experience them being enthusiastic, happy, proud, and enjoying their professional career is as good as it gets and a great reward for any leader. It was their individual contributions that made our company successful, and that made it an honor and a pleasure to be a part of. It is about serving people, and it is very gratifying being part of a team's success, no matter the mission.

44

## Feedback

I once read: "The truth does not change based on one's ability to accept it." Such a great statement that is truer than true!

Feedback is one of the most important items in the leader's toolbox. It's difficult to lead by sitting behind a desk or looking at a computer screen all day, because you just don't discover things you need to know about your company by doing that. You can watch the world go by sitting at your desk. I know you have probably heard, "You don't know what you don't know." Make the effort to communicate with people beyond your desk. Doing so will supplement your own knowledge, create relationships, and motivate the team.

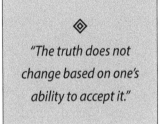

*"The truth does not change based on one's ability to accept it."*

I watched a friend, and leader of a fortune 500 company, walk around and have conversations with people almost as if he did not have anything else to do but talk with them. He knew them, their families, and their interests, and he remembered what they had previously shared with him. He asked questions about them, their well-being, and about their jobs. Of course, he had plenty to do, but he understood that spending time with his employees was important to them, as well as his awareness of their concerns, and therefore to the success of the company. Feedback is something you should seek, not avoid.

In the book *In Search of Excellence,* by Tom Peters and Robert Waterman, they wrote about MBWA—Management By Walking Around. I thought, *I do that! Where did I learn to do that?* From my grandfather, who went all around the building talking with employees, almost every day. My dad was a little different in that people came to him. Sometimes, however, I thought things were happening he did not know about—or enough about—things that I believed he should know. I made a mental note: *I'm not going to do that. I'm going to do what my grandfather did—walk around.* I made it a point to seek out people to learn other viewpoints and perceptions. Getting people to share their realities shows you care, and giving them the opportunity to know their leader helps retain people in the organization. What I did not understand was that my dad, with his open-door atmosphere, had so many people coming to him that he actually knew more than I'd imagined. How that important interaction with people is accomplished can differ, so long as it is part of the leader's work habits to be in touch, not out of touch.

Feedback is vitally important, and leaders should view it in a positive manner, whether it comes from interacting with people or in a more structured interface. The ability to receive and interpret the information received will determine the value of feedback to the recipient. It helps you to understand that your views are not the only ones—even when you think they are. You need to move away from what you think you know to find out what you need to know. You need to understand that you can be wrong, and have the ability to accept and understand that. Your view of the way things are may not be what others in the organization are thinking, and that is good information for you to know. Feedback, unless it is from an unreliable source, is a commendable device, and not a sign of weakness. If feedback is honest, sincere, and

*Feedback, unless it is from an unreliable source, is a commendable device, and not a sign of weakness.*

presented properly, it facilitates understanding and situational aware-ness. Ask yourself: *What does someone else know that I need to know, even if it is just an opinion?* The exchange should be shared communi-cation done the right way, and everyone must be willing and strong enough to learn from the input.

Do all leaders use feedback? No. Some are the my-way-or-no-way (or my-way-or-the-highway) people, and others just do not trust their associates enough to appreciate their input. Does that necessarily lead to failure in leadership? The answer is probably no. However, they are missing the information and other intangibles that come from feedback. Additionally, they are not establishing relationships or a trusting organization through good use of feedback. So, you can hold on to the "I am right" belief until you fail at whatever is involved, or learn how to deal with input. Feedback can be a driver of ideas, infor-mation, opportunities, and other important things for any organiza-tion, and therefore leaders should work to establish an open conver-sation environment in which ideas and honest discussions take place every day. The exchange of content is more meaningful if shared in a positive, person-to-person manner.

Often a leader will have a trusted person who he or she goes to for information and counsel. A CEO friend called that having a "Longstreet" person. That name came from General James Longstreet who was the person General Robert E. Lee went to for advice and strategy. However, Lee rejected Longstreet's advice at a very critical moment in time. Having a trusted, dependable associate can be a valuable resource to a leader no matter the type of organization or endeavor.

I was pleased to have the opportunity to be a confidante of the CEO of a leading company and one of our business partners. (I am certain I was not the only one.) Our relationship, fostered over many years, was such that I could be honest with him without jeopardizing our relationship. "Tell me the truth," he'd say. His point was that leaders need to hear the truth rather than what people think the leader wants to hear. He was getting enough of that already. Inherently, leaders have opportunities to both give and receive feedback, and it is valuable both ways, because it is the sharing that makes it worthy. It is easy for people to avoid the truth when communicating with the boss because they are afraid of any consequences that may come from that communication. The CEO would tell me how much he appreciated the input and sharing of beliefs, information, and ideas.

Frequently, by the time information gets to the boss, it has become somewhat distorted. Any type of incorrect information supplied to the decision maker can exacerbate the leader's difficulty in making good decisions. Distorted, unreliable information, or even a lack of information, can cause blind spots, all leading to misguided decisions. Feedback is intelligence that can help you make better decisions, so the credibility and reliability of any feedback is important for you to understand in order to properly use the information acquired.

President Lincoln gained reliable feedback by going to the battlefield thirteen times to talk with the troops as well as the officers and gained firsthand knowledge, which he most likely would not have learned otherwise. This was the same man who filled his Cabinet with high-level people from the opposition, most of whom did not agree with him, or even each other. They were known as the Team of Rivals. He listened to their input intently, even though they rarely reached a consensus among them. But, in the end, a consensus did not matter, because he was the one ultimately making the decisions and taking full responsibility.

To add to the line of feedback, I intentionally relied on our managers to keep me informed on things that could make us more successful. It was so important to know what, in their view, was needed and what they thought was possible. They were the ones charged with making their areas of the firm profitable and successful, so they knew better than anyone what they needed to grow our business. They saw opportunities that were out there for the company, and I encouraged their input.

Obviously, not all feedback is critical in nature, but it must be valued and treated with respect for it to be beneficial. Admittedly, there are leaders, and even organizations, that do not want to hear the truth or anything negative that does not agree with their view. Such a position or environment is not positive and is not on the right path toward beneficial exchanges. As I said, hanging on to your viewpoint without being open-minded is not a strategy for success.

Let's be clear: good feedback is different from gossip. Feedback needs to be factual and based on the truth. Talk around the water cooler is gossip, and probably not worth repeating. To take gossip a step further, people who talk about others in a negative way are only doing damage to themselves, not the subject person. People quickly lose respect for someone when that

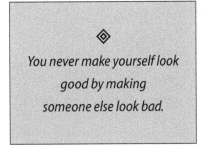

*You never make yourself look good by making someone else look bad.*

person talks negatively about someone else behind the person's back. You never make yourself look good by making someone else look bad. If someone feels the need to vent, they need to vent up to their supervisor, not laterally or down to their subordinates. That type of venting is part of the problem, not part of the solution, and it is destructive to the venting person and to the organization.

I learned midcareer to use the vigorous question, "What do you think?" It builds trust, value, and confidence, and I used it all the time in both casual and business conversations. People appreciate the idea that someone else might appreciate their thoughts. You can use this question as often as possible when communicating with and directing people. Ask, "What do you think?" It is a way of saying, "I would appreciate hearing your concerns." I made it a point to say, "It is your decision to make, but here are my thoughts—what do you think?"

Here a caution is needed. Using "What do you think?" in group discussions, or in actively seeking feedback, does not mean installing groupthink, where the thinking of the organization as a whole takes on the beliefs of a group. Seeking input and feedback is rooting out the issues, ideas, and needs, and ultimately finding out how can we do better. Worthy feedback, done well, is to discover the creative

---

*Worthy feedback, done well, is to discover the creative thinking of individuals, to share ideas, viewpoints, and knowledge for improvement given openly and in a positive environment. But ultimately, the decision responsibility remains with the leader.*

---

thinking of individuals, to share ideas, viewpoints, and knowledge for improvement given openly and in a positive environment. But ultimately, the decision responsibility remains with the leader.

If negative, damaging feedback issues arise, do not table them, but do your best to resolve those in a timely way, because those underlying, unresolved issues turn into problem generators. The longer negative issues linger, the worse they become, and the more difficult they are to resolve. The best method for resolving troublesome issues is to work toward eliminating blame, fear, and guilt to keep things calm, and to create a can-do attitude about what needs to happen.

A lesson learned was when we had a brother and sister both on our team. We valued both, but the brother became a negative influence with his immediate team members. I was hearing about his negative talk and behavior frequently. Because of his sister's presence, and because I didn't want to upset her, I allowed the problem to stir way too long before taking corrective action, which resulted in the dismissal of the brother. Unfortunately, I was taking some undercurrent heat from some of the team for allowing this situation to linger. I knew what had to be done, even though it was not the easiest thing to do. I waited too long to make the decision on the brother, causing the team to question their confidence in my leadership. These issues cannot be addressed symbolically; they need to be positively resolved, curing the problem in a timely fashion.

## Communication

Great leaders must be excellent communicators.

There is no way around it, because to lead well, you have to be able to communicate well. Not all people can communicate effectively. It is a skill set which those in leadership roles need to work on continually if they are not naturally good communicators. Clear communication is a powerful tool for inspiring people, gaining trust, and aligning efforts in the pursuit of the firm's common goal. Effective communication of the organization's direction, plans, culture, and so much more is what leaders must do in order for people to follow enthusiastically. A leader's communications should be honest, clear, and transparent; expressed with empathy and caring; and give a sense that you understand your audience and their goals, as well as those of the organization. People watch your body language as well, so it is not only about choosing the right words, but also using the right manner, tone, and presentation style. Any form of communication that makes people roll their eyes or develop negative feelings or thoughts should be circumvented. How you make people feel with your communication can enable confidence and positive attitudes.

*How you make people feel with your communication can enable confidence and positive attitudes.*

You need to know that, to a large degree, you are the one responsible for them understanding your message—no one else. Accordingly, organize your sentences so that they can be easily understood. Avoid ambiguity, and take care not to overpromise in communications, because both of those can come back to haunt you if the message is not reasonable and clear. A good thing to do is fact-check your ideas before writing or verbalizing them. The style, content, and vocabulary need to be appropriate for the intended recipient.

A leader's words and implications can travel fast through the organization, and people tend to repeat the leader's message word for word. Words, after they are said, are difficult to correct or take back. That was one of the early mistakes I made, and it led to a teaching opportunity for my dad. In a group of our sales staff, the conversation was about a company in our industry that was doing very well. Without thinking anyone would take me seriously, I said, "Don't worry about them, we are probably going to buy them." As it turned out, they did think I was telling them the truth, not joking. The word got out, not only in our company but also went to the company I referenced. This was not a good moment for me at all. The result was a closed-door, very direct, serious confab with my dad that sticks in my mind almost every time I open my mouth. It was, as he said, a never-again lesson! Sometimes what you say in a not-so-serious manner can become serious to others, even when it was not intended that way. The more important your role is, the more careful your communications need to be, as you simply cannot make off-the-cuff comments.

Communication is an essential information exchange on which all organizations rely every day. It affects every part of the organization, at every level, keeping everyone moving toward a common goal. Effective communication is both internal and external with business associates, the community, vendors, and takes place in many forms for myriad reasons. There are more communication channels available now for leaders to use both within and outside the organization, and all should be used properly and effectively. Communication keeps those responsible for getting things done informed and in sync with desired objectives and outcomes. You want to have everyone on the same page, and good, clear communication makes that happen. It allows greater understanding at all levels, helps build teamwork, and enhances employee satisfaction.

In past years, the majority of communication was by letters. Today it is email and text. Those two are quick and easy. The caution is to avoid misunderstandings, which can occur in an instant with these two methods. Try to construct your communications from the viewpoint of the recipient to ensure you don't create something you did not intend. How the reader interprets your message is crucial. You cannot win a text battle, as it becomes a lose-lose exchange.

I don't see how you can achieve your goals, or maximize your opportunities, without constant, relevant, truthful internal and external communication that is not overly guarded, restricted, or discouraged. However, the guidelines do not change because it is internal or external communications. Try to imagine any company functioning without effective communication and you will understand why that company may not be doing well. To be effective, you should create an environment of trust, truth, and transparency using all the methods for communicating. Companies that permit employees to speak the truth will function more effectively and peacefully than those that don't. An environment that permits the acceptance of people speaking openly results in better coordination, better workflow, and the results will naturally be better.

The firm's managers and people must talk with each other frequently to have the ability to develop and share ideas, plans, and work processes. It is the responsibility of the leader to allow and ensure that communications are working well both within the company and with external contacts. Properly executed communication management, to the best extent possible, prevents misinformation from becoming a problem. No doubt, false information can be harmful if not controlled or addressed in a timely way. Obviously, you do not want to restrict good communication while dealing with untrue issues. Communication management also helps set the manner and tone people use in their communications with each other. Realistically, people prefer to be talked *with*, rather than talked *to*—there is a difference. Good in-person communications demonstrate respect for the receiving person. When the receiver feels respected (and not defensive), they are much more likely to receive and understand the intended message.

There are times when communications can be critical of leadership and difficult to hear. I have tried hard to separate criticism from helpful input, and it is not an easy thing to do. When critical comments arise, it sure helps to think maybe it has some validity, and maybe it is justified. If it is communicated fairly and accepted well, it can help things become better.

When I was young, sometimes when needed, my dad was direct about my performance; and without a doubt, I took some as criticism rather than positive advice. After a while, I was able to understand that his intentions were well meaning, and that he was probably right, and was being a mentor, not a judge. The key was to change my thinking, because his counseling was important, well intended, and would help me improve. What is the difference between criticism and mentoring? It can be in how you accept it. I may not have always achieved the objective, but learning how to accept his counsel made his advice more palatable and helpful. The change that worked for both of us was in me, not him.

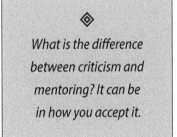

*What is the difference between criticism and mentoring? It can be in how you accept it.*

Criticism seems to come with the job of leader, and how leaders handle criticism mentally is part of what they learn to do. There is going to be someone, somewhere, who does not like your leadership. The world is not perfect, so understanding there will be some disagreements out there, and suitably dealing with them, will help leaders to be successful. Leaders learn constantly, adjust, and grow with their experience and acquired learning. In their leadership role, they also need to be somewhat flexible in their methods and make adjustments to achieve positive, meaningful outcomes. Learning how to accept and use, or not use, criticism comes with personal growth and experience in the job.

As best as possible when communicating, make judicious use of the two dangerous words *never* and *always*. *Never* is not always *never*, and *always* is not *always*. If you say you are never going to let certain things happen, and then you do, creditability is lost in the eyes of employees. Neither can you promise to always do something, because things change, things happen, and *always* falls through a hole. Further, using *always* and *never* can lead to an argument about whether something really is "always" or "never." That discussion detracts from the intended point of the conversation. Be careful about promising results that are suspect or marginal in their accomplishment. The words of the leader take on more importance than those of others who are in similar circumstances. Sometimes a person's mouth is engaged before their brain is in gear, so to speak.

*The words of the leader take on more importance than those of others who are in similar circumstances.*

Make sure you think it through before the communication begins, because your people will hold you accountable. I learned a long time ago: you can't talk first and think later. It is the other way around.

To me, a vital part of "down the channel" communications is continually telling your constituents how much they are appreciated and that you value their work to the company. Continual praise and reinforcement keeps people motivated, enthused, and on the team.

## Practice Listening

Great leaders are good listeners and take the time to listen.

Listening is a skill and, unfortunately, a skill too many people lack—and they don't know it. If you are not good at listening, and you know you are not, then it is something you need to work on if you are going to be effective as a leader. There are jokes about God giving us one mouth and two ears for a reason—because you need to listen twice as much as you talk! But the basic thing to understand is that it is my turn to talk, and then your turn to talk—without interruptions. To be a good listener, you need to be an engaged, open listener; listening skills can be developed to become a habit, but you have to work on it. Good listeners are open to viewpoints of others without judgment during the conversation. Asking questions after allowing an individual to express their interest, concern, or story, becomes part of the developed good listening habit.

I was once invited to be part of a lunch group of ten businesspeople who met regularly for discussions and sharing ideas. (There are a number of these types of groups to participate in if you are interested.) I received a phone call from another business owner who was also a fellow church member, who asked if I could join a business discussion lunch group once a month. This group included seven men and three women, none of whom I knew previously. Two of the participants had a bad habit of interrupting the person speaking after almost every sentence with questions, which in most instances, would have been answered if the speaker had been allowed to finish their points! This made a three-minute spiel twenty minutes long, and often took the conversation away from the speaker's intended point. It was annoying and became so frustrating the group gradually disbanded. No one believed bringing the issue up to the two individuals would have changed their behavior. I was sorry, because there were some good exchanges of ideas emanating from our gatherings.

In that same vein, one person should not go on a twenty-minute monologue either. Speakers need to make their messages concise, without dominating any conversation. It is certain that one begins to lose the attention of the others at some point in over-talking on any subject matter.

Stephen Covey said, "Seek first to understand before you seek to be understood." The truth is you cannot add value to anything you do not understand. Listening is a physical act, the sound should lead to hearing—that is, understanding. Sometimes people are present for the whole conversation, but do not really hear the meaning of the conversation because they have not made the effort to truly listen.

*To learn, you have to listen more than you talk. Good listening is when you hear, understand, ask questions, and learn.*

I have seen so many people looking at their phones, typing on their computers, or doing other things while in the pretense of listening. That behavior tells the person talking that you are not interested in them or what they have to say. It is demeaning to both parties, really. It becomes a sure way for the person talking to lose respect for the "listener."

No doubt, there are instances where the listener's wheels may be turning during the conversation, which can make listening a difficult skill to master. We all have encountered people who are already thinking of their answer or rebuttal before the speaker has completed their thought. They want to control the conversation and only value their position. Frequently their auto-response is the exact opposite of what you are saying, or even denial of any truth in your statement. They are not good listeners and are not benefiting from the conversation, because they are not really hearing the presenter. In addition, if you are the one who is doing all the talking, then you are not a good listener either, because you are also not listening. To learn, you have to listen more than you talk. Good listening is when you hear, understand, ask questions, and learn.

I learned a lot about listening from my grandfather, who did it better than anybody. When someone was talking with him, he'd frequently put his foot up against the edge of his desk, clasp his hands together, and look right at the person. He listened as long as the person wanted to talk, and when he spoke, it was calmly and firmly, with wise counsel. Some said they went to see him to complain, but during the visit would forget what they went to see him about. He let them talk it out, and when they came out of his office, they were happy.

When someone comes to speak to you, you should immediately stop whatever it is that you are doing and look at them with your undivided attention. I promise, whatever you were doing will be there waiting for you when your visitor leaves. Not only is this a great listening skill, it is respect, and it creates trust and value.

I am not sure I have ever seen anybody be as effective a listener as he was. He likely knew that understanding is often more important than solutions. It was amazing that he was so firm, yet also so skillful with his communications, as he spoke softly but wisely. You do not need to be loud to be a leader. Pay attention—you may be surprised at the information and even meaningful questions you have after being engaged in listening.

## Sharing Results

Author Jan Carlson said, "An individual who is given information cannot help but take responsibility."

When I first moved into a sales manager role, none of the financial results were shared with any person below my dad, my uncle, and the CFO. The managers had no information to measure against other than the vague, "You did well." I absolutely hated that, and was able to talk Dad into making the change to share the appropriate financial information. I convinced him by saying the managers just need financials relative to their group, perhaps not the total numbers. It worked. You cannot expect managers to achieve good results unless they know what their goals are, how they are preforming, and what the results were. You cannot effectively manage something if you do not have measurements by which to judge. That is why they keep score in a ballgame. It is a determination of success, and you will not know the results of your efforts if there is no measurement that is known and shared with the participants.

Measurement of results should be a tool for improvement, not blame. There is significant accountability in the financials; however, performance improvement is the fundamental goal. Yes, sharing is also a matter of trust in the individuals receiving the information, and that confidence is incumbent with the team leader's job. A lot of useful, actionable information is contained in the numbers, and that information can be put to work by the appropriate individuals when shared in a timely and open way. So much of business now is data driven, and decisions are made based on that data. The key to effectively use the data lies in the ability to interpret and understand the knowledge and numbers generated. Once that information is understood, the essential next step is to effectively put it to use.

A good leader knows how to define success with measurable shared results and appropriate information, and numbers play an important role in determining success. All of which is to say that the more appropriate information you are willing and able to attain and share with the right employees, the better the results will become.

Everything cannot be a secret in your work environment. Leaders need to be open and forthcoming with information, because a closed-information environment will cause morale, attitudes, and behaviors to decay over time. There is much that cannot be shared with employees, such as payroll, HR, and legal—but there is also much that can and needs to be shared, like plans, strategy, marketing, success stories, and more. Secrets are usually not a good thing, and they will become a bottleneck if that is information that people should know and need to know. A leader attempting to keep the bulk of information and knowledge wrapped up in his or her mind is damaging to the success of the organization, because no one person should, or even can, hold all the information. That is a closed-information practice. In any organization, good, reliable, actionable information is paramount, as the more you have, the better you are able to perform.

Unfortunately, some leaders believe disclosing and sharing is risky, and therefore hold back too much, which can result in serious consequences. Trust, confidence, performance, value, pride, and more are lost. It is far better to share and gain the benefits and outcomes, which come from making open communications a trusted practice within the organization. Ray Dalio, in his book *Principles* reinforced this, calling it "radical transparency" and saying, "you have nothing to fear from the truth."

You don't want your employees to say, "We don't know where we are going." This is obviously not a good working environment for any organization. If you don't know where you are going, you are not going to get where you need to go. Without knowing where the organization is going and the "what" and "how" of the plans to get there, the team can make only limited contributions to overall success. Show them the map. Open and transparent communication with your entire organization is a necessary habit for consistent performance.

## Delegating

An important part of leading well is knowing how to delegate well.

That means you need to know what to delegate and not to overuse or underuse it, because there is a delicate balance in either over- or under-delegating. Too much is not good, and too little is not good enough. Delegation is so much more than giving someone something to do; it helps create a trusting relationship by giving people enough space to use their skills and deliver results. It shows that you have confidence in the recipient of the delegated task to accomplish his or her responsibilities. Both micromanaging and not delegating are bad leadership practices—there is no other way to say it. You cannot do everything, and the more things you feel you need to touch, the worse workflow can become. Not to mention the respect you lose from your people by not trusting them. People want, and thrive on, the contribution their efforts make to the whole. Trusting people's skills is prominent in successful companies.

*If you do not believe in your people enough to delegate to them, you will not enable them to develop and become the people you need them to be.*

If you do not believe in your people enough to delegate to them, you will not enable them to develop and become the people you need them to be. You cannot be fearful that the job will not be accomplished properly if it is not done by you. Neither can you be afraid to delegate because you are concerned about giving up some amount of authority. If it is a competency issue preventing you from delegating, then train someone or hire the right person so that you can trustfully delegate. Delegation moves the decision-making process down the chain and frees time for the delegator, and it is much easier accomplished if you trust the individual. It is the responsibility of the leader to have capable people to whom you can shift duties that are not yours, but theirs, to perform. Give them the information, teach them if needed, set the expectations, and then let them do the job. This will improve productivity, both for you and for others. Assign the work, and trust individuals to use their skills and allow some reasonable mistakes in the process. As Henry Ford said, "Failure is the opportunity to begin again, this time more intelligently."

While I am discussing mistakes, I think three types of mistakes occur which are treated differently. One is simply the mistakes made by all of us in our everyday efforts. They are honest mistakes like processing errors, or forgetting call backs—these things are just going to happen because we are human. Unless people are doing absolutely nothing, they are going to make mistakes. Next are the learning mistakes that can be made by someone because they do not have enough knowledge or training relative to the job requirements they are preforming. Those create teaching opportunities to enable the individual to do his or her job correctly, and not repeat the mistake. The last are the unacceptable mistakes that get you off the bus: dishonesty, theft, or mistreating a customer or fellow worker are a few examples. Leaders should allow for learning mistakes, but continuous inexcusable mistakes require timely solutions.

In delegating, you can get more from people by using respectful communication. Often this is simply a matter of asking rather than telling or ordering. People do not like to be ordered around. We have hired people to a leadership role who used very direct communications, which amounted to rough orders rather than a respectful approach to their fellow employee. It sometimes took encouragement, counseling, and some amount of training to get them to change their approach to managing people respectfully and trustingly. It becomes important how leadership input and guidance is exercised so that trust in the leader is not blemished, but guidance is given and accepted positively.

When people are micromanaged, they believe they have lost the trust of their leader, and they will most likely believe they have also lost their value to the organization. If and when that happens, it can have a negative impact on their job performance and satisfaction. Success depends on having the structure and environment in which you can trust the team members. If you don't trust them, you may have the wrong people, or actually the problem could be you. Look in the mirror: Are you a trusting leader?

*By far one of the most important things you can communicate to someone is that you trust them.*

It is incumbent upon the leader to manage the attitudes of the people, no matter where the people are in the organization. If you can positively affect a person's attitude, you can positively change their job performance. I continue to stress the importance of attitudes because it influences all of a person's actions. If attitudes are positive, then results are good. By far one of the most important things you can communicate to someone is that you trust them. If that relates to accomplishing a specific job or task, then it is even more meaningful. What you do not have, in their mind, is the responsibility of doing their work for them. So, do not fail at your job by trying to do someone else's job. As writer Ken Blanchard said, "People who produce good results feel good about themselves."

Many years ago, I had gone to one of our VPs and said, "We have a job that needs to be done, and I will help you get it done." Knowing we had a good enough relationship so he could speak openly, he said, "Mr. Smith, this is what you pay me to do—I don't need your help. What I need is for you to let me do it for you." If you have the right people and they are worth their salt, the last thing they want to hear from their boss is, "I will help you do this." People want to be trusted to do their job without unneeded help from you. Leaders need to be careful not to cross the line between teaching and interfering, because it is easy to get out of your lane. Again, in the mind of the worker, working with does not mean doing their job for them—to them, it means being valued as a team member.

Occasionally, people who have moved through the ranks to become a leader often have difficulty letting go of their previous roles. They still want to be part of the group, do some of the work they used to do, and have the freedoms they once had. Much of that activity needs to be left behind, and they need to realize they are now a leader, not a worker. Sometimes in life you have to give up something to get something. That change requires giving up previous responsibilities and the discipline to execute new responsibilities. A transition from doer to leader compels you to make entirely different decisions, with new responsibilities, and work at an entirely different level. In his book, *Good to Great,* author Jim Collins related that the leader must drive the bus, and not be a passenger. If you have moved up, you are no longer a passenger. You use the knowledge and experience gained from the previous job, but that previous responsibility is no longer yours.

In our company, we had a few good lessons on delegation. In the first, the department manager in our company, who led twenty plus direct reports, had chosen to go to his people almost every morning to tell them that he was the boss. Obviously, this was not a good practice, and on my walk around the office his reports told me about the issue. I asked this manager to come see me. When he came, I asked who was responsible for scheduling the workflow of his department, who approved vacation times, who approved promotions and pay increases, who was responsible for the results, and who was responsible for hiring and terminations. He responded he was responsible to all my questions, and he hoped I knew this. My response was that I did know, and so did every one of his subordinates. I told him he did not ever need to tell his people he was the boss. He needed to stop this behavior because he was losing the respect of his employees, and some were even thinking of leaving.

Bottom line: if you are doing your leadership job correctly, the last thing you need to be concerned about is your people knowing who the boss is. Everyone knows who the leader is, you just need to perform like a leader, because that is what those reporting to you want and what they expect from you. You earn respect, you do not dictate it.

The second example occurred some time ago when I learned that our call center people were having difficulty knowing how to handle certain customer call situations. I had instructed them to handle the customer's total needs from A to Z without having to ask for help, transferring the call, or calling the customer back. They said they were unsure of their authority to handle some customer situations, which had previously been a manager's decision to make. I told them they were empowered to make a decision they thought was the right solution for the customer and the company. If it turned out to be a wrong decision, they were not going to be in trouble with me, but they would learn from their mistake and it would likely not happen again. It was not about the ability to hold them accountable for judgment errors, because authority was given. This change in empowerment worked very well, because it made it easier for our people to do their job, and easier for our customers to do business with us as well.

Learning from mistakes is the important thing, while not learning from them becomes another mistake.

People will be more confident and aggressive in meeting their delegated responsibilities if they understand their role and the empowerment associated with the role. It allows people to utilize their skills to help the organization perform better. Allowing for that success or failure is part of delegating the decision-making process, empowering employees, and building their skills and confidence. The call center lesson not only improved the work environment and empowered these employees, but it also showed my trust in these individuals. Their confidence and job satisfaction went up noticeably.

*Learning from mistakes is the important thing, while not learning from them becomes another mistake.*

The third situation happened with a service manager in our

company many years ago. As talented as he was with equipment repair and knowledge, he had difficulty managing the service department. His method was to move around the department each day, checking on the progress of the techs. When he found someone who was having difficulty with a repair, he would take over and do the repair himself. The problems resulting from this should have been obvious to him, but in spite of numerous counseling efforts, he simply could not bring himself to change his habits. Productivity was dropping, he was missing teaching opportunities, and his leadership tasks were not being accomplished. I was a sales representative at the time, and all of us were fielding customer complaints about the slow repair times in our service department. Ultimately, my dad had to terminate this man's employment. The manager's failure to delegate hurt not only himself but also the productivity of the techs, the performance of the service department, the development of his employees, and the respect from his reports. Even the performance of the company itself in the eyes of our customers became somewhat suspect. This was a prime example of poor delegation skills, attempting to do someone else's job rather than yours, and the consequences associated with that behavior.

Lee Iacocca, the former president of Chrysler, said, "Hire great people, and get out of the way." There are so many great leaders who are proponents of this mantra. It does not mean that you are giving up control or leadership. It sounds like an oxymoron, or contradiction, but it is not. It is giving your people the chance to be successful, and that is the antithesis of micromanaging.

# Chapter 4

## A Leadership Scenario

*Who is driving this bus?*

You are going to be the bus driver—a **leader**. "Who said I am **capable** of driving the bus?" The ones who taught you how to drive—**education**—and the company that hired you—**trust**. The bus is going to go where you steer it to go—**direction**. But you can't just drive it wherever you want to go; you must have a determined destination—**goal**. You can't drive the bus around in never-never land, because you have to have a route—**plan**. You need to have the **vision** to see what is on the road in front of you as you go. There are some things—**work**—that you need to do on the way, to get where you want to go—**results**. You need to make stops and get **people** on the bus—**hiring**—and let some off the bus—**firing**—and make sure they *fit* in a seat that is a good place for them.

You can't keep the money they pay; you need to be **honest**. It is not your money; it is the company's money to keep the buses running—*sustainability*. Also, you can't just keep some of their money because you think you deserve more, you must have *integrity*. People are counting on you to be *dependable* and be *on time* for them. You can't miss a stop, or be late when you are supposed to be there. Your people and the company *trust* you to get them where they need to go. You need to *respect* your riders, so you need to be a good person—*character*. Nobody wants to ride with a jerk. You need to *care* about that lady who needs help getting on the bus. People appreciate that you *care* about them and their needs. You need to *communicate*, keeping everyone informed about where the bus is on the route—*plan*. You need to say *thank you* to your riders—*employees*—for riding the bus, because they could have chosen other means to get where they want to be.

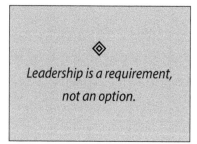

*Leadership is a requirement, not an option.*

You need to *listen* to understand your riders—*employees*—and know what is happening on the bus. You are *responsible* for making sure the bus is running well. The company will hold you *accountable* for all these issues. If you do these things, you will earn the *respect* of your riders—*employees*. If you are not sure—*self-aware*—that you have the *passion* to drive a bus, then you shouldn't be a driver—*leader*.

Leadership is a requirement, not an option.

# CHAPTER 5

## CHANGE

*Change is constant.*

Change is a move from the status quo to something different or better.

Sometimes "the way we do things" becomes a little stale, and that is when you need to ask, "What if?"

A leader is responsible for ensuring that their organization is doing the right things at the right time and keeping the company on the right track. They need to be able to identify the necessary changes and the right time to make those changes. Change entails both internal change and external change, which can come from outside opportunities.

Many things change—people, the business, the economy—all this drives the need for change and adjustment within the organization. It is tempting to think you will reach a point where you can sit back and say "we did it." But no, you cannot become satisfied or complacent.

You are never done. Will Rogers, the humorist writer and commentator, famously said, "Even if you are on the right track, you'll get run over if you just sit there."

You simply cannot wait for things to become painful or destructive before you initiate needed changes. We recently saw an airline company wait too long to update their software and the entire company shut down for a costly period of time. I have seen companies wait too long to replace a sales representative and lose customers in the absence of a sales person. You need to continually think about what might work better, or more importantly, what is not working, in an ever-changing environment. What are the possible disruptions taking place that need change? The objective is to improve; therefore, you need to make the best efforts to change as fast, or faster, than the changing market. To achieve improvement, you have to have change. They are mutually dependent. That should mean, in addition to the known changes, you have to keep innovating and looking to the future. The look forward may reveal more than was originally anticipated.

*To achieve improvement, you have to have change. They are mutually dependent.*

Define the change, and work toward setting the boundaries around the changes to be accomplished. What is going to be changed, and what will not change? Change and consistency are strange bedfellows because both are

*Change and consistency are strange bedfellows because both are needed, making it a peculiar challenge to manage both concurrently.*

needed, making it a peculiar challenge to manage both concurrently. The challenge is that you must maintain consistent delivery of your efforts to your base while executing necessary changes. Operational changes are not easy to accomplish, as people generally do not like changes in their work structure.

Having gone through a number of these types of changes, I found that managing change was sometimes difficult. Change leadership and buy-in came from both internal and external resources. You need capable, trusted people within the organization to lead and facilitate changes. There are also very good, knowledgeable outside resources, such as consultants, lawyers, accountants, and technology experts, that can be equally important and helpful in the change process. All of this was certainly true each time we needed to change and update our operating platform. That kind of change takes time, training, managing the employee acceptance of the new routines, supervision, and a great deal of effort from everyone.

However, you cannot be afraid of change and need to be confident in your ability to employ change and do it successfully. Education, learning, and experience are all catalysts for good outcomes in a changing environment. There's no question that change does involve some risk, and you should not expect that you can remove all risk. That said, I think if you fail to properly plan for change, you are basically deciding to fail in the process. So once you decide the outcome you want, then you need to focus on what processes are necessary to achieve the outcome—then execute the plan.

Change management is key to achieving good results. Preparation, planning, supervision, and getting that buy-in to the process are some of the keys to making change work. You should work to create positive energy in your teammates around the need for making changes.

Employees might resist change because the reasons behind the need for change are not made clear. The explanation for change, or the "why," needs to be followed by the details of how, when, and by whom the changes are going to be accomplished. That is just good change management. You should pay close attention to comments during any change process, not only to maintain a positive environment, but also to learn what the people involved are thinking, and what they can contribute to the desired results. "If you want to know how to do something, ask the person doing it," goes the saying. Some things may not be what you want to hear, but giving people the opportunity to share their insights into the ongoing change process can improve the results.

# CHAPTER 6

## THE RIGHT THINGS

*Doing the difficult things right.*

Think about it. If you do something that is difficult and do it well, you will take pride in your accomplishments. If it was easy, you probably would not think twice about it, as there would be very little sense of accomplishment. The joy is in succeeding with a difficult task. Or, as author and management consultant Peter Drucker said, "Effectiveness is defined by doing the right things well." A basic starting point is for a leader to know what the right things are. You need to know the sources of success and how to use them. Unfortunately, I have seen some leaders who just don't have a good grasp of what the right things are, or even what needs to happen next. Two things that are important for a leader to understand: first, what good is, and second, what the right things are. Not only should you be doing the right things, you should be doing things right.

> *You can bet that our company did not grow more than fourteen times over by doing the wrong things. We became an award-receiving, respected, trusted distributor in our business by doing the right things—by knowing what the right things were, doing the right things well, and doing the right things at the right time.*

You can bet that our company did not grow more than fourteen times over by doing the wrong things. We became an award-receiving, respected, trusted distributor in our business by doing the right things—by knowing what the right things were, doing the right things well, and doing the right things at the right time. Plus, all of that has to be consistent over time. We did those things, not just here and there, but in every aspect of our company by employing and trusting the best people who did the right things well. These were things like dependability, consistency, integrity, customer focus, and industry support. The credit goes to the managers and employees who cared enough to make it happen.

So, what are the right things? They are the things which enables the organization to be successful. It should not be difficult to determine and understand what those are. If you do not know, then that itself is a problem. The things can be divided into two parts. One are the factors you need to do to perform well, and the other are the critical success factors, which you absolutely have to do—no exceptions. The critical factors are things which will make you successful if you do them, or not successful if you don't do them. They are the make-or-break, win-or-lose factors.

Those critical success factors are not the same in all circumstances, and sometimes that knowledge requires more effort to determine. Thinking the organization through—from operations to customers—will provide the answers. What means the most? When you know and understand what is critical, you can move forward on the right track.

In our case, the right things began with our customer-focused strategy and always asking what mattered most to our customers. We then identified what we could do better than the competition and what new capabilities we could add, which were not yet in our industry. We added a call center to make it easy to do business with us; an on-site mobile service repair; same-day order shipments; a repair assistance and consultation telephone line; customer education classes (STI University); and an online information and sales website. A number of operational improvements were made as well, like accounting efficiencies, workflow changes, warehouse operations, and IT updates. Often things which may have been courageous or innovative at the time become standard operating procedure tomorrow.

I often called one of our business associates for a job hire recommendation, and if he liked the person, he would say, "He knows what good is." This is such a telling statement, because, sadly, many people simply do not know what "good" is. They have never been at a place, or level, to experience it and don't recognize it. If you do not know or understand what good is, then you are not going to be able produce it! You simply do not know the standard you need to

> If you do not know or understand what good is, then you are not going to be able produce it! You simply do not know the standard you need to meet.

meet. Suppose you were competing in the pole vault and you thought setting the bar at eight feet was good, then clearly you would not be competitive. The record pole vault height is well over twenty feet. Sometimes people and organizations think they are good enough, when they are not. Their lack of awareness of what good is just does not allow them to be good. Taking it a step further, sometimes even good is not good enough—best is the best! However, I stick by the basic conviction that you have to know what good is, what it looks like, what it performs like, and how to produce it.

So, how does one become aware of what good is? Certainly one way to recognize it would be by numbers that reveal performance. However, I think you see good more clearly in service delivered, visual recognitions of great results, high-level performance, comparative judgments, and success stories. It is an observation factor, and should be as easy as "You know it when you see it." The reality is that you have to be good to recognize good and to construct good. When you see and experience good customer service, when you see a great work of art, when (and if) you walk on the course at Augusta National, you recognize what good is. Regardless, many people simply do not get it, are not able to produce it, or do not apply the standard in their own efforts.

*Know what good is.*

You would be amazed how many times I have used and shared "know what good is" with people who had never heard it before. I have been working with a very large organization for over a year now on a major project. In one of the first meetings concerning the project, which was about hiring the prospective person to lead it, I told the group, "The right person needs to know what good is, because if he doesn't know what good is, he is not going to be able to produce it." The group excitedly jumped all over the statement. "We have never heard that—that is great." Now they are repeating the statement often and using it in other discussions.

I heard football coach Nick Saban say something that I interpreted as: there are things which you choose to pay less attention to, which is different from things you need to focus on. I related it to business and thought the reverse was also true. I have observed leaders who choose to ignore, or put on the shelf, something very important to an employee, or even the organization. To them it becomes somewhat out of sight, out of mind. Leaders need to be able to understand and choose the important things on which to focus. They also need to know what things they can pay less attention to, because making the wrong choice on critical issues can be damaging. Know where your focus needs to be and what is important for a successful outcome, and make the right efforts to make it happen. Outcomes are the result of the process. So, it becomes important to know what to focus on in the process, and what things are less worthy of attention.

For example, years ago, our main competitor was a mediocre firm. They were good, and believed their performance was satisfactory. But we saw the opportunity to raise the bar, and began doing the things that were needed to allowed us to achieve a higher standard of performance and customer satisfaction. Each of our managers had great ideas, and I was able to add a few of my own. We were raising the competitive bar while our competitor remained satisfied with their structure and go-to-market methods. To our benefit, they were unable to understand, or were not aware, that the bar had been raised.

They were not paying attention to what was important. Like the frog in water becoming increasingly hotter, they were on auto pilot and did not see it. A few years later, they sold their company, and in a few more years, it went completely out of business. They had set their bar too low for what was required, and their inability to understand the new level of goodness facilitated their failure.

Leaders, and leading companies, must always look like a leader, act like a leader, perform like a leader, and, to the extent possible, show no weaknesses. You need to "walk the talk" of organizational leadership, and consistently good execution is the key to success. The industry leaders will include the smartest, most responsive, and best companies in executing their goals and objectives.

# CHAPTER 7

## STRATEGY

*Your plan for being the lead dog.*

Organizational strategy is the sum of an organization's plans and actions. It is the vision and the associated "how to" of the go-forward plan.

Strategy is very important to any organization because it is the response of the company in terms of where money will be allocated to meet or create demand. Strategy is also a response to the competitive activities in the market. For progressive companies, the goal is to be a leader in their field, if not *the* leader. "If you are not the lead dog, your scenery is not so good," as they say. If you want to be the best, strategy will be the "how to," or the plan that will get you there. A strategy is not the goal, it is the process to achieve the goal. It can be part of the responsibilities of the leader to guide the "how we are going to win" ideas and platform. The victory usually goes to the competitor who can outthink, out-plan, and out-execute others. Locating, attracting, and retaining customers is the purpose.

Strategy is the plan for the future intentions of the company. It is the map of the "what, how, why, and by who" by which the organization will continue to exist.

There are myriad considerations in developing your strategy, including market decisions, products, services, economics, relationships, resources, core competencies, and growth. None of the strategy tasks are easy; they take a lot of thought, effort, and time to develop. *What are we going to do, and how we are going to make it work?* Developing the plan requires you to know what the right things are to include, what the opportunities are, what changes (if any) are needed, and how to execute all this knowledge in your strategy. You need to know and understand for whom the strategy is intended—*Who is the target?* You need to know what your resources are, and how to best allocate your resources to achieve the tasks outlined in the plan. A lot of the considerations need to be around *How do we get it right?* because failure will be expensive. What is the protocol?

Organizational strategy is thinking ahead about the competitive platform, which you use to shape your future, and you want the plan to competitively work in your favor. Planning may need to involve how you are going to make it to market with what you have, because additional resources are expensive. While it is easy to get consumed by the more immediate thinking, you have to include an equal amount of time on the long-term goals as well, because it is a master plan for the organization which includes both short-term and long-term goals. Additionally, much thought needs to go into the capabilities of the people who will be responsible for achieving the outcome. That planning is centered around what assets are in place, or are needed, to allow the tactics of the plan to be accomplished. All of this is so important because you want to win, and success must be earned, it is not achieved by accident! I once told a community college class that was visiting our company for the day this concept in very simple terms: "Culture is who you are; strategy is how you do it."

A good communication plan needs to be determined so that everyone involved is reading from the same page. It will require consistent and timely communication as the execution evolves. Strategy thinking never stops, and some of it just evolves over time. Sometimes it is not a totally new approach; it is instead an update, or revision with new ideas, products, services, capabilities, and go-to-market methods. It may be as simple as a new perspective that makes the plan work. The changing market reality is what requires companies to continuously refresh their strategy. In addition, there is no doubt that strategy changes accompany, or hopefully occur before, the market dynamics occur. Often an accelerated market movement can require the leader to make almost instant decisions to stay competitive. Remember, you are not playing by yourself in the marketplace, there are others out there.

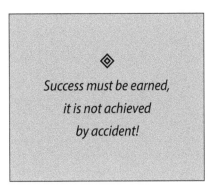

*Success must be earned, it is not achieved by accident!*

When it comes to leadership, remember:

Do the right things.

Do the right things on time

Do the right things right.

Set the standard, change the rules, be the leader.

# CHAPTER 8

## LEADERS VERSUS MANAGERS

*Leading and managing are not the same.*

Not everyone wants to be a leader because of all the commitments and responsibilities that come with the job. A leader guides people and the organization, while a manager directs and manages people and tasks. Or, stated differently, people follow leaders, but they work for managers. Leaders work in a macro basis and direct what *should* be done, and managers work in a micro basis and direct how things *get* done. Very basic, but true. Some functions do overlap, but the primary job for each is different.

Leaders set the direction and create an environment for managers to meet and achieve the desired goals. They make decisions at a higher level. Leaders have less to do with controlling; that is more a manager's role, because they are task-centric. Trusting and empathetic leaders let managers, within parameters, design and do their jobs.

# Some Things Don't Change

The important common denominator to both roles are the people responsible, because they are the subordinates who carry out the work to completion. So, included in the leader's job description would be establishing the vision, driving change, strategic thinking, influencing people, making decisions, and establishing the culture. Leaders set the company's overarching direction, they stand on the bow of the ship, looking at the horizon for possibilities. Leaders need to consider the future, pair that with the way the company is functioning currently, and then communicate with both managers and employees. Leaders see the future as they want it to be because they are able to see the big picture—vision—and set the path to be followed.

Managers are responsible for interpreting and executing the leader's vision and carrying out the applicable functions, so managers are task- and process-oriented. Their duties are outlined in their job description, and have specific jobs they need to accomplish. They are responsible for getting things done the right way, and their job is mostly in the present tense—the here and now. Managers make things happen a step below the leader, with items such as productivity, process, timelines, training, implementing changes, assigning job tasks, and managing the execution. Their thinking is more tactical and purpose-driven.

In some cases, the size and complexity of the organization can determine how much separation of responsibilities there is, and needs to be, between a leader and a manager. Clearly, the number of people in the organization, as well as the number and locations of offices, play a part in this. When we had fifty-eight employees and two locations it was much easier than today, with our 280 employees and twenty-one locations in four states. More locations, more managers, more people.

However, the same difference of responsibilities remains between the two jobs, no matter the physical separation or organizational size. Overall, effective operation depends on understanding where the separation and boundaries are between leading and managing and keeping them separate.

There needs to be effective two-way communication between the leader and managers, because without proper communication between them, the functionality of the organization suffers. It is the job of the leader to set priorities and ensure the managers are focused on and accomplishing the right tasks and job functions. That takes communication.

During our company's reorganization, I went from being a sales manager to CEO basically overnight. With that change, I was attempting to be a manager and the leader at the same time. I was involved too deeply in too many things. I was too deep in the weeds, as they say. One day, two of the VP/managers came to me and said, "Mr. Smith, you don't need to be doing some of the things you are doing." Wow. That caught me off guard. The VPs said, "We would like for you to move the management of these things to us so you can do what we need you to do." That was embarrassing! I *thought* I was doing my job correctly. But I was not.

By trying to be a manager and the leader at the same time, I was not letting the managers do their jobs effectively, and I certainly was not empowering or helping them develop as good managers.

After that meeting, I did exactly as they requested and moved the tasks to the next level. It was a principal learning experience in leadership for me, and one I saw more clearly from that point forward. Good, talented, effective managers are critical to workflow and task accomplishment. They keep people motivated and ensure things are accomplished the right way, the first time. Organizations function better when good managers are in place and empowered to do their job.

In this regard, there is a work-life and personal-life balance that is important to achieve. It took a while for me to grasp the need for balance. For a number of years, I did not take a vacation. Today, I look back on that time with regret of not being more aware of the need

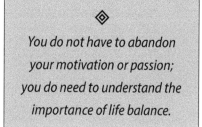

*You do not have to abandon your motivation or passion; you do need to understand the importance of life balance.*

for balance. The time I dedicated to my business took away from time with my family. I thought I needed to be the first one in the office and the last one to leave. Being a workaholic is not necessarily an aspirational goal. Mental health, physical health, and personal happiness are more important than your career. You do not have to abandon your motivation or passion; you do need to understand the importance of life balance. Please understand that you can put in extra time, go the extra mile, and work harder, but you can efficiently get the work accomplished within reasonable boundaries. At this point I think the verdict is still out on remote work in terms of effectiveness and life balance. There are both positives and negatives inherent in the environment, and many of the issues will take time to resolve.

# Part Two
## Culture

# CHAPTER 9

## DEVELOPING A GREAT COMPANY CULTURE

*Culture is a set of attitudes, standards, shared beliefs, values, goals,
and practices that characterize any organization.*

Culture affects everything an organization does because it is what you do in the workplace. Leaders need to understand the power a good culture can have, because culture has a direct relationship with results. Culture is who we are, how we do things, and what we stand for. Culture is not the same as a strategy, but it is part of it. Clearly, culture begins at the top and trickles down throughout the organization; therefore, shaping the organization's culture is primarily the leader's role. It is critical that you have not only a good culture, but also the *right* culture, because culture is who you are.

Culture is intangible, but you can see it, hear it, and feel it within virtually any company. Every organization's culture is unique. An organization's culture is on display every day to its employees and all the way to the customer. Everything counts, and everyone notices. You can tell if people enjoy their work, their work environment, if they are respected, trusted, and if the leadership is honest, moral, and truthful.

Culture has a direct relationship with results.

The overall culture of the company needs to be a cornerstone in the framework of the organizational purpose, and therefore culture and strategy need to be aligned. The message is: "We are here to win by doing things the right way," meaning people work together through teamwork and mutual respect in order to meet the established culture goals.

It is better not to be building the plane while flying, so define the culture up front, and communicate it widely. In the process, think what would work best in your organization and establish the policies, expectations, programs, and standards to match your goals

Recruiting and hiring the right people for the organization is one of the primary factors in developing a good culture, because they are the ones who live it. In any organization, the right people with good attitudes make the path to establishing a good culture significantly easier to accomplish and sustain.

A very recent correspondence from one of our employees stated: "The culture comes from the top. In my years, I have worked for many companies that culture and leadership is nothing more than words and the performance of the team reflects this facade. You all truly set the example and walk the talk. I am very thankful to be a part of the STI team!"

The culture of an organization becomes its image, both within and without. It can drive the spirit of the enterprise to excel in its sphere. Culture drives attitudes, behaviors, and thoughts, and it governs how people interact with each other. It is a positive motivator for the members of the team, because they understand and appreciate what a good and positive environment means to them. I recently saw the results of a survey that determined culture was 10.4 times more important to people than the organization itself. It is, after all, where they are, what they contribute to, where relationships occur, and where success is achieved. A large part of your life is spent at work or in the working environment. Any good culture is one where expectations are high, communications are clear, transparency and trust are encouraged, and is a clear reflection of the organization's management style. The right culture is a basic yet significant factor in successful companies, and it sets the foundation for becoming a great company.

I think that in most every organization's culture, there are strengths and weaknesses. There are also companies that are defined by a toxic culture, and people are very aware of which companies those are. The quality of their people, the job satisfaction of their employees, the unethical manner of their business conduct, and other issues make it abundantly clear to everyone just what they stand for. That reputation precedes them everywhere, and certainly can be a negative influence in their dealings. These are dysfunctional companies with question-able leadership, and they tend to be less successful than companies with a positive culture.

Often in companies with toxic cultures, the leadership of the organi-zation seems unaware of the realities surrounding them. They must be looking at themselves through the wrong end of the telescope, so to speak. Beyond poor leadership, some negative corporate cultures simply occur by accident, with no intentional development toward what they want to be. Without a doubt, a toxic or adverse culture can bring down an organization, and that alone is a compelling reason for any organization to address a detrimental culture. All companies are different, but a conspicuous common ingredient is the requirement for a good, positive culture. It is real and is essential in creating successful companies.

The adherence to policies, beliefs, and actions driving a good corporate culture has a proven record as a basic fundamental asset in better-performing companies. The employees of those firms have much higher employee job satisfaction rates and staff retention. The good culture of these organizations becomes a mindset and is reflected in the positive attitudes of the leadership and people. However, there are times when good culture policies are documented and verbalized, but adherence to those standards is not properly maintained and enforced. It is not good enough to just state the desired culture, you have to drive it to make it work. So, a good culture is not an absolute, and even inclusion of the basic good attributes will not constitute a one-size-fits-all culture program. Every organization has to understand what fits their situation and work toward that goal. In order for it to be a reality, it must be well defined.

Cultures can evolve and change over time, and even in well-established organizations it can deteriorate if not maintained. People know what is important, and if the rules are not clearly defined and enforced, they begin to feel disconnected with fellow workers and leadership. If accountability is not practiced, and actions not taken to reinforce the proper behaviors, people are negatively impacted by the absence of good management.

Top-performing companies talk a lot about culture to ensure both the importance and relevance of their work environment. They treat their people respectfully. They stress the value of each job function and give meaning to the work of each employee. They are good with internal communications and share the organizational values and purpose. The bigger your organization is, the more frequently you need to express the organization's values. Less in-person contact with leadership generates the need to use other means of communication to maintain good organizational culture. It is much easier to share beliefs and expectations in smaller companies because of the daily interactions of those involved. Culture gives everyone in the organization a sense of pride, promotes teamwork, drives attitudes, and influences work performance. Strategy changes with the times; culture should not. Organizational identity and culture become the reality to all involved with the organization, and this corporate identity and reputation strongly influence the compa-

*Strategy changes with the times; culture should not.*

ny's overall success. To a large extent, striving for cultural excellence can and should be a habit, and not an insincere act. For that to happen, leaders themselves must exhibit the right standards every day. I don't think you get any days off from that.

Everyone who came into contact with my grandfather, for instance—from employees, to suppliers, to friends—knew his integrity, morals, and heart. Reaching back to 1925, he started a legacy of leadership now in its fourth generation—an established culture lasting generations. Thankfully, not much has changed in maintaining his values. Our organization is based on honesty, integrity, caring, a good work environment, dependability, and a focus on the customer. I am not sure there is one word to adequately encompass all this, but it is the "who we are." Companies take on the look and feel of the leader, and as such we strive to live it daily. As with many decisions in life, when there are too many choices, focus can be lost on the basic important ones, so we work hard to not let our focus on culture dissipate. We have maintained a work-family environment as a consistent and valued part of our beliefs and style. Our company is important, but it will never be as important as your family. That belief drives the culture development process to have a strong focus on people because they are the core of any organization.

We are very proud that both our good culture and success are well known throughout our industry. It is important, achievable, and does not happen without intentionality and work. Recognition of a good company culture resides both internally and externally through communications that are transparent and engaging of corporate values and purpose.

# CHAPTER 10

## PROTECTING YOUR CULTURE

*Keep your finger on the pulse.*

Once you are able to establish a good culture, you darn well better protect it. Excellent companies protect every detail of their culture, down to the smallest item. You simply cannot compromise on any part of your culture or your reputation. People pay attention to what leaders watch, and therefore leaders who pay attention to the many aspects of the organization's culture will ensure that this culture takes on increasing importance. As with personal self-awareness, corporate self-awareness enlightens leaders on where the company's environment stands. You should take time to ask yourself often, *Are we really who we say we are? Do we stand for the things we say we stand for? Do we like what we see? Is our behavior consistent with our beliefs and stated objectives?*

To protect the desired culture, make a commitment to living it and making sure that it runs throughout the entire organization, from top to bottom. Those efforts also need to be persistent in protecting and perpetuating that environment so that over time it does not erode. Not that it will become irrelevant if neglected, because a company's culture will always remain relevant; it just will not be what it needs to be, and it will be relevant in a negative way. An organization with a toxic culture and reputation is not on the road to success. In simple terms, not correcting the issue will simply perpetuate the wrong issue, and that is not something you want to allow.

An example of how we protect our culture at our business came when we first set up our call center. One of our new customer service individuals cursed out a customer who was placing an order and was disappointed we were out of stock on an item he needed. We have several solutions for handling out-of-stock occurrences, but he chose to curse at the customer, and then said, "What the h*** do you want me to do, make one?"

The customer immediately called me. I was down the hall from my office when my assistant came and said, "I think you really need to talk to this customer." When I did, he repeated the conversation to me, word for word. I apologized to the customer, thanked him for caring enough to call me, and told him that the entire order that he placed would be free, and we would get the out-of-stock item to him ASAP. I then walked to the call center, collected the individual, and dismissed him, explaining to him the reason for his termination. Cursing and being disrespectful to anyone is not justified in any situation, work or personal. He was out of the building fifteen minutes after the original call.

Was this an overreaction on my part? I don't think so. It was the right thing to do. He made a "get you off the bus" mistake. Interestingly enough, the other people in the call center said, "We don't know how you found out, but we were going to tell you, because we know that behavior is not acceptable here." There have been similar occurrences over the years that get others off the bus, but fortunately there have been very few, and all justified. People learn quickly what the expected behavior is. I don't curse and don't see the need to do so, or what it adds to the conversation. I guess this is one of those attributes of my dad and grandfather that benefited me, and more importantly, I do not model that type of behavior to our people, or anyone else for that matter. Issues are going to happen, and keeping them under control the right way is a basic element of a consistently well-performing culture.

People want to be associated with organizations with good reputations and good cultures; they take pride in such an environment. Just as important customers enjoy doing business with companies with strong reputations and good cultures. Think about the comfort level you have when you are dealing with a trustworthy, reliable, well-performing company—it is just better.

The CEO of one of our major suppliers, on his first visit to our company, came into my office and said that he could just feel the positive work environment when he walked into the building. He said, "Your people enjoy being here—no wonder you guys are so successful." This was a great compliment to our culture and to the employees who make us successful. Which, to me, confirmed that you should also listen to what people on the outside are saying, because perception tends to become reality, externally. Protecting your culture never stops, and you cannot rest on your laurels. It is an everyday effort, and you cannot let it slip to the back burner.

# CHAPTER 11

## COMPROMISING THE CULTURE

*Don't let your culture be compromised.*

I had multiple opportunities to compromise our culture to secure business with customers, and even with a vendor, by conducting business outside of the culture.

Years ago, the then manager of our largest customer called me to ask what was in it for him personally if they continued to do business with us. I was shocked that being in his position with his organization he would even ask. My answer to him was that was not and never had been how we managed our company, and we would not even consider doing anything close to what he was asking. I told him even if it would mean the loss of our relationship with him and his firm, we would not engage in any under-the-table activity to gain sales.

We actually did lose some of his business to a smaller company that did participate with him in a dishonest manner. Fortunately, this unethical manager did not stay long in his position, and we did not compromise our integrity to gain the temporary sales associated with his behavior. Reflecting on the culture passed on to me, I understood deviating from integrity was not something we did, no matter the size of the issue.

There were other times when we were approached to conduct business unethically, but the answer was still the same. No matter how good the short-term gain may look, once you break the commitment to your principles it becomes easier, or certainly tempting, to do it again as the temptation swells to repeat the activity. If you are willing to break the rules, you are essentially stating, "The rules don't apply to me." It is difficult to keep the lid on compromising situations from occurring in any organization, and your reputation begins to take a hit if those types of situations are not tightly controlled. In the long run, it is not worth compromising the established organizational culture, not even once. Somewhere, sometime, the truth will surface, and the consequences will most likely not be good. Some organizations do not survive the kind of negative exposure resulting from events that compromise the culture.

# Chapter 12

## Culture Change

*Adopting a new mindset.*

It is definitely possible to make a change in an organization's culture when necessary. The first thing you need to understand is the need for change, because a culture change will be a behavioral change in the organization. You need to look for and be able to see and understand the existing truth to affect change. Once you understand the need for a culture change, build a clear and compelling vision of what you want the culture to become. You have to establish the desired outcome you want, and then focus on the changes required to achieve a better culture for the organization.

In the fall of 1984, initiating our reorg, we had two locations: our main office and a small branch facility with only three people. That made it much easier to begin a culture change. Our company culture was good, but we recognized the opportunity for some positive behavioral change. Communicating value and trust, as well as expected performance standards, to everyone was the objective.

It may sound like a small thing, but one of the first things I changed was the Christmas party. I wanted to send the message that some behavior at past parties was not acceptable. I knew that my dad was in favor of the changes because he had tried to get his brother to do them. We invited all our retirees, my family, and my brother's family. We chose a local charity to support and invited a minister to give thanks and share a prayer. We gave out awards, we eliminated alcohol, and we sang Christmas songs. It was a special event that felt good to attend, and it sent a message of family, morality, and integrity.

I began the event by telling our people we were successful because they were the best, and each and every one of them was important. To instill value and pride, we told them how much we appreciated their work and how much we cared about them. It was a great opportunity (but not the only one) to say thank you. We wanted them to feel like a family and part of a winning team.

We set the bar high for performance, cooperation, attitudes, working together, and taking care of our customers—all part of a culture that we wanted to be "who we are." Today, we have twenty-one locations in four states, 280 employees, and while it is somewhat more difficult to convey the message when you're so spread out, it can be done if you make it a priority.

I discovered a long time ago the four Ls: live, laugh, love, and leave a legacy. I had this stuck on the refrigerator door so I would see it every day. We are all creating a legacy to leave behind in our personal lives, and any business is doing the same. To me, organizational culture is an attitude as well as standards, because if it is good, it is understood and reflected by everyone in the organization. It shows itself in their performance, personal behavior, and well-being. So if change is required, a succinct, well-defined culture outline should be prepared to establish the goal. It will be difficult get there without a clear definition of who you want to be. Once those decisions are made, it needs to be enacted with strong, clear communications to all concerned.

In some of our advertising for the company, my brother included the statement, "Many things change, but fortunately some do not," referring to our basic corporate values. You can definitely apply the statement to leadership skills and methods, as the basics of good leadership remain true, regardless of the need for evolving leadership methods and effectiveness. However, with hindsight, the different generations of Boomers, Gen X, Millennials, Gen Z, the Covid pandemic, remote work, and supply chain issues all drove huge changes and some unprecedented challenges to work habits and the business environment. There are a number of benefits which workers like. However, there remain some questions yet to be answered, such as in-person learning, team building, idea exchanges, and advancement opportunities (out of sight, out of mind). Work places will look different, robotics will be more prevalent, and some jobs will be done by part-time professionals. One day, this period of time will be a case study for business schools everywhere. What happened? What was good, what was bad? What changed? What could have been done differently?

# CHAPTER 13

## SUSTAINING YOUR CULTURE

*Once the right culture is established, it can be perpetuated*
*by everyone in the organization.*

To maintain a strong company culture, you need to be willing to look at the culture and adapt changes as necessary, because companies evolve and change over time. Therefore you have to make sure the values which define the company's success are in alignment with the existing internal and external conditions. When people know what the standards are and what is expected of them, they will influence fellow team members, as well as newcomers, to hold them accountable to the organization's behaviors. This is peer pressure in a good way. If it is a winning attitude, and one of success, they will communicate that to all, both inside and outside the organization. They do it because they take pride in the company and enjoy being part of its success. Maintaining a strong culture then becomes a team effort understood and embraced by all. People buy in to the shared values and practices of the organization and become involved in protecting the work environment.

Many times, when two companies come together, the good culture of one can replace or improve the culture of the other. When we purchased another company, I was told by the company's manager that the people in their company were saying things like, "We may have done this in the past, but we are not going to get by with that at Smith Turf. We need to step up our game." This is culture reputation working in advance in a positive way.

For years, North Carolina basketball coach Dean Smith had a four-part culture message he consistently stressed to his teams. This message was: "Play hard, play smart, play together, have fun." To which I say: work hard, work smart, work together, have fun.

# Part Three
## People

# CHAPTER 14

## PUTTING PEOPLE FIRST

*Employees are the backbone, strength,*
*and success of the organization.*

The employees of any company produce results through the work they perform. People represent the knowledge as well as the experience resident in the company. Each of their skills is an important contributor to the whole, and to be successful they must be consistent in their performance. It is through their efforts, skills, communication, and ability to work together that the company will be successful or not. Working toward a common goal, they carry out the mission of the company. If you are a people-focused company and put people first, it translates into a more successful company.

Football coach Vince Lombardi once said, "I will not have an average team." What a great statement and such a strong position to take, as it showed the importance of the individuals and how much he valued the players. He told the players each of them was there because Green Bay believed they were good enough to be there. If Green Bay did not believe that, they would not be in the locker room. The better the people, the greater the organizational success will be.

*A business is only as good as the people.*

Probably my strongest business belief is that a business is only as good as the people. It is true for any organization, any size, any place, any endeavor—no exceptions! Being only as good as the people means they are only as good as the weakest link (person) in the chain. They have to cover or make up for the weak person, requiring them to divert their efforts to achieve the tasks. It also seems true to me that the better the people are, the better *you* have to be to lead them. Great people, together with great leadership, becomes a great company, which produces great results.

Think of good teammates like this: if you were picking "dream" partners in golf, you probably would pick Tiger Woods, Jack Nicklaus, and Arnold Palmer. You want to go to work every day with the best, and I had the privilege to do that. At a convention, I was sitting with the national sales manager of the host company when he said, "Wayne, I can pick out the STI people as the crowd goes by—they stand out. They present themselves better, they are articulate, and they are smart. Few companies here have one guy that is as good as any of yours." High-quality team members are vital to any successful organization.

One of the principles Coach Dean Smith often stated was that if you put the best team on the court, you should win. A very simple, yet achievable objective, and his success demonstrates the direct result of using talented individuals as the foundation for a team. Coach Lou Holtz said, "You have to have great athletes to win." These basic concepts are applicable in sports as well as in most all professional endeavors. Neither of those are aha revelations, so why is it difficult for some organizations and leaders to get it? The sad fact is that not all leaders or companies recognize the importance of employing quality people.

The importance of employing good people cannot be overstated. People are the most valuable asset that you do not own.

Frequently people ask about how our company became so successful, and I'll say, "It's the people, they are the best." To get those great people, you should never be afraid to hire someone who is better or smarter than you, no matter their level in the organization.

> ◈
>
> *The importance of employing good people cannot be overstated. People are the most valuable asset that you do not own.*

One day, I got a note from the director of sales from Toro after his visit to our company, part of which read, "I was quite impressed with your new facility. It not only is one of the finest Toro distributorships that I have ever visited, but the attitude and the enthusiasm of your employees was something that became apparent the moment I walked through the front door."

When the comptroller of our company left, I spoke to our CFO about the candidates he was interviewing for the job, and told him to choose someone who was as good as, or even better than, himself.

He later said that guidance helped him make his choice, and it turned out to be a good decision. Hiring is the genesis of achieving the goal of creating a winning organization with the right people. The recruitment and selection process is your opportunity to predict the potential of people, so start there mindfully and carefully.

Remember, the draft and transfer portal is always open in the business world, as well as the sports world. Talented, skilled people will always have outside opportunities available to them. Talented people can find job functions available to them, which they have the skills to fulfill. Therefore, organizational leadership has to be performed well, at all levels, to keep the team together, and lead them in the right direction. Loyalty in today's world is difficult to attain, and it takes effective leadership and favorable work environments to achieve a degree of loyalty to the organization.

*One of the ways to generate employee loyalty begins with understanding what motivates people—what means the most to them.*

One of the ways to generate employee loyalty begins with understanding what motivates people—what means the most to them. I continue to stress the importance of building trust in the organization. Organizational trust starts with the commitment you build with each individual. Trust and value are numbers one and two on my list of what employees value most. The work contribution and personal satisfaction associated with their job is paramount to their attitude, job satisfaction, and performance. Their personal value to the organization plays an important role in an employee's decision to stay with a company, because it is high on the list of what they care about. The importance people have, and feel, toward contributing to the organization's success is something that leaders can control, and need to promote. Talented individuals, when given the opportunity to use their skills, make companies better.

Employees also need to have a good understanding of the purpose of the work they are responsible for producing. Knowing why they are doing something and what the results of their efforts will be is just as important as how to do it. Understanding the "why" is easy to communicate, and goes a long way to better work performance and job satisfaction. During the "why" communications, take time to listen to your people about their concerns. You will learn a great deal. Not all of it may be work-related or positive; however, the act of listening to them, and clarifying the "why" of things, lends to better results in the work environment overall.

People are the heart and soul of the organization, and they should be treated as such. As their leader, you cannot overlook the responsibility you have to them. As part of that responsibility, you need to build them up, care for them, and hold them responsible. It is almost unnecessary for me to say that it takes the work of all associates individually to make the company successful. Together we achieve more. The collective responsibilities between the leader and the team as they all work toward a common goal will determine the success of the organization. People in the organization are equally, if not more, important than the customer. On this note, I have a firm, long-held belief: the better you treat people, the better they will treat your customers. It creates a "pay it forward" atmosphere. As a matter of fact, you can probably take it a step further: the better the staff are treated, the better the relationships will be for everyone associated with your organization, inside and out.

One day, I sat in the back of the room during a presentation on the five levels of leadership. Level one was the base, and level five was the highest level of leaders. On level five were names we all recognized. The presenter said, "We all probably know a level-five leader, and as

*The better you treat people, the better they will treat your customers.*

a matter of fact, one is in the room on the back row—Wayne Smith." Wow! Shock! That caught me by total surprise. My first thought was, "Thank you." But, immediately, my second thought was that it was not about me, I don't deserve the credit, it's about our people. It is not "me" it is "us," because they are the ones who make our company a success. They had the responsibility to make it work, they were going to make us successful—and they did. I think our great people made me look good because I got to work with the best team. They made us successful, and any win was for the team. You may have heard the metaphor, "When you are riding down the road and see a turtle on top of a fence post, you can bet he did not get there by himself." That is the way it is for our organization, and the way it should be in great companies.

I referred to the Golden Rule as a guide on how to treat and deal with people. It was Dad's method both within the organization and in his personal life. "Do unto others as they might do unto you" is a great starting point. Professional leadership is embedded with mentoring, opportunity, support, trust, and more. The fundamental standard is caring for people. Dad and Granddad were there for you, and everyone knew it.

Dad's thoughtfulness reached both inside the company and outside as well. Like the poor family he found on a back-country road with four kids. The entire family barely had clothes or food. I went with him many times to take them clothes, food, and at Christmas, a carload of presents. Like the people in the neighborhood near our office who could not afford heating oil in the winter. Dad paid for several big oil trucks to fill every home's oil tank in the neighborhood.

My granddad took into the company a mentally challenged boy—Howard, who lived with his unemployed mother—to do odd jobs around the building to earn money. His jobs were opening the mail, cleaning, and believe it or not, getting on a city bus and taking money and checks to the bank in a paper bag. You could do that back then. The way Howard looked and behaved, no one ever thought of bothering him, and he would go and come. He did that for years without a single problem. Granddad paid for all his needs and helped his mom with her rent and expenses. Howard even got a paycheck. When my granddad passed away, Dad took up Howard's care. Howard was a joy; everyone liked him and realized and appreciated what was being rendered for Howard. Being part of something like that is so gratifying, particularly if it is caring and comforting, as it was for Howard. It became a source of pride for people that everyone in the company cared for and looked out for Howard. The feeling you get from helping someone else is truly rewarding. Regardless of what the help is, big or small, it is worth every ounce of the effort. It is so fulfilling that at times I find myself looking for those opportunities to be helpful.

As a leader, you have to have empathy for each individual, show you care about them and care for their well-being on the job and outside of work as well. They will never forget how you make them feel. That demonstrated personal interest and care has a significant positive impact on people. If you treat employees like family members, with respect and concern, the work environment improves and it will have positive results. People believe in you if you believe in them!

# CHAPTER 15

## HIRING WELL

*Getting the right people on board.*

When recruiting and hiring, you must be intentional about looking for people who meet the standards required to be part of the team. Since hiring is where you start building a team, a good understanding of the qualities you are looking for in a person should be determined from both professional and personal aspects. You are not going to be 100 percent correct in all hiring decisions, but it requires your best efforts, because bad hires are expensive to correct. You also have a responsibility to the person's family when they join your team, because their work compensation supports more than just the individual.

Jim Collins's book *Good to Great* did a terrific job explaining not only the value of people, but their job placement as well. He did that with the analogy of a bus—you not only need to have the right people on the bus, but you also have to get the right people in the right seats. Remember, you're not just trying to fill the seats, you're trying to fill the seats with the best, and *right*, people. The objective is putting people where they can maximize their potential to be successful. If a warm body is all you are looking for, that is all you are going to get. Collins also emphasized the need to get the wrong people off the bus.

*Personal attributes are so very important, because if someone is not a good person, you are not going to be able to make them one.*

When recruiting, the first thing you need to look for is someone who is genuinely a good person. Personal attributes are so very important, because if someone is not a good person, you are not going to be able to make them one. It took me longer than it should have to figure out that even with my best effort, I could not make a person into something they were not. Further, you cannot change someone if they don't want to change. I have to admit, I still hold an underlying belief that I can do it.

Hiring is somewhat of a gamble. A manager whom I hired had a very direct, demeaning, hard approach to his reports, and some were leaving the company because of his harsh methods. For a short period of time, I coached him on supervisory methods and relationships, but with little results, and he continued to boss people around. This person had almost everything required to perform his job, except the relationship skills. I even enrolled him in classes and paid for them myself. Nothing worked, as he just could not change. His termination was difficult because he had potential, but it was the right thing to do for the company. Originally, he looked very good and seemed to be the right hire, but ultimately, he was not. The correct answer was not staying with the wrong person. Hiring has some risk, and making good choices is not easy no matter how hard you try.

Once you find the right person, you can teach them the job, your products, your services, and your business. You hold them accountable for the performance standards of the company and give them the resources and the opportunity to be successful.

Attitude is one of the most essential attributes a recruit must have, because of the impact attitude has on their performance. It may not be the most important attribute, but it must be a consideration when evaluating any candidate. Some years ago, a survey revealed that 85 percent of people's skill/success was dependent on their attitudes. As Albert Einstein said, "Weakness of attitude becomes weakness of character."

*Once you find the right person, you can teach them the job, your products, your services, and your business.*

In the work environment, leaders as well as managers have the responsibility of stoking positive attitudes. This is why my grandfather walked around the company every day, and why a leader needs to talk with and get to know their employees. I said earlier, as a leader or manager, one-on-one communication provides an opportunity for them to know you. These exchanges show them you care and give you the opportunity to share the organization's vision and direction with them and how vital that worker's role is in the company's success. Attitude governs people's approach to all aspects of their lives— personal and professional. Attitude has deep roots and is something a person brings with them from their life experiences. It influences relationships with fellow team members and affects their work performance either positively or negatively. A positive attitude leads to greater happiness, productivity, health, and success, and plays a big role in their perception of their job. People with positive attitudes are the ones who will be integral to the team's performance, as they are more successful, personally and professionally.

Look for someone who is motivated and has the desire to succeed. We know it is very difficult to make people do what they don't want to do, so they need to possess not only the right professional skills, but also a good work ethic. Experience has taught us that even one person with a bad attitude and work ethic can negatively influence the entire group. Those behaviors and attitudes manifest themselves in many ways—complaining, poor work performance and habits, no interest in improvement. These are all indicators of a problematic employee. The sooner those situations are corrected, the better. Not only are they negatively influencing others, they are also creating dissatisfaction with leadership if leaders fail to properly deal with the issue in a timely manner.

Recruiting for the proper fit needs to be at the top of the list when considering a candidate. To work, a person's personality and attitude need to fit with the existing culture of the organization. The right person to have on the bus must not only be capable, or more than capable, but also must clearly be the right fit for the organization's culture. I receive many comments from employees about how well everyone gets along, supports each other, and how much they appreciate the positive work environment. That does not just happen. It is intentional, and it starts with selecting the right people.

Do they have a good work ethic and motivation? Will the current employees accept this person, and will the individual be a good team member? Will the candidate be able to meet the job performance standards of the organization's expectations? Can this person be successful in the job for which he or she is responsible?

Bottom line: business success is about valued, motivated, skillful people.

## CHAPTER 16

## HOLDING PEOPLE ACCOUNTABLE

*An important part of good leadership is*
*holding people accountable.*

People need to be accountable not only for their work performance, but also how they conduct themselves in the work environment. Holding people accountable will create trust between team members because they know they can depend on one another. Additionally, it means they are responsible to the organization and others for their actions. They are responsible for, and expected to meet, the goals and standards and obligations inherent in their job performance.

Personal relationships between a leader and employees can be a difficult to manage, yet productive, part of being a leader. If the interaction is handled professionally, it can be a benefit and underpin the ability to work together. Problems develop, though, if this intervention becomes an overly personal, or an involved, close relationship with someone for whom you are responsible. In that scenario, it can be challenging to have some needed leadership, discipline, or mentoring conversations. When those close personal friendships occur, it can make it difficult to do what you know must be done as the leader. Accountability is much less difficult to achieve when there is not an overlying close relationship between a leader and a direct report.

However, you do need to have relationships with people—just not the kind that would prevent you, as the leader, from holding them accountable should the need arise. You just cannot display or have favoritism in managing your staff because others are watching your leadership behavior. Showing favoritism will negatively affect how you are viewed as a leader, and will result in a loss of trust and confidence from others. This kind of preferential treatment might be promotions, work assignments, or even work habits like excusing someone for being chronically late. This activity is easy for people to notice and can definitely take a toll on motivation in the workplace.

Regardless, you must hold everyone in the organization to the same standards. To do that, you have to treat everyone fairly and mean what you say. Do not say anything in these circumstances that you are not going to follow through on. You have to handle the direct report accountability issue correctly and in a professional manner without creating blame in the process. Holding people accountable involves setting clear expectations and also understanding their work perspective. Feedback moves both ways during the communications in order for it to work well.

There are significant consequences, legal and cultural, related to the methods involved around holding someone accountable. Enforcement and discipline with individuals must be handled correctly in order to avoid mistakes that get you in trouble. Refer to the standards, document the conversation, clearly describe the issues, do not debate, and do not get emotional. There is an element of learning in these sessions, but most are about behavior and failures. It is easy for the conversations to become a back-and-forth event, and that is not what needs to happen. It is not a debate forum, so don't let a defensive person turn the conversation into that situation.

Any discipline certainly must not be conducted in front of or around other people. That would be demeaning to the person being spoken to, damaging to the person's respect and relationship with others, and cause a loss of respect for the manager. Making someone accountable is a private matter, and should be handled as such. In most cases, it is better to have an HR staff member, or another appropriate person, present at the meeting when this takes place. Additionally, any other personnel issues should be addressed often enough to ensure that when reviews take place, performance issues should not be a surprise to the individual.

As consultant Dann Harris said, when the need arises to make changes with a person, it can be accomplished in one of three ways: transfer (recasting), training, or termination. The choice depends on the individual and the situation. In terms of training, I have found many times that people can be very resourceful if you give them the proper training and resources and the freedom to use their skills. When I invested in them and demonstrated I had trust in them, they frequently excelled beyond my expectations.

# CHAPTER 17

## MANAGING INDIVIDUALS

*Every person is a unique individual, and therefore*
*you likely need to manage them in different ways.*

This is another case where the one-size-fits-all rule does not apply. When managing people, you can manage them individually as long as you use the same set of rules and standards that govern the organization for all. Managing individually means you must know the person, what is important to them, what motivates them, and target guidance directly to any issues they may have. Knowing the singular needs of the person allows you to lead on a more individualized basis. Working with someone in this manner can bring out their skills and allow them to become more productive.

One of our managers began giving two assistants a full week's worth of tasks at one time. One could work her way through each assignment methodically for the entire week. The other would come back at the completion of each assignment for the next assignment, regardless of having a full week's worth of assignments. The manager was a little concerned about this, so I talked with her about the benefit of managing individuals differently. She continued giving the one who could handle it a week's assignment of work, but to the other one she gave a job at a time, rather than a full week, and the change worked. There were no changes in the rules, no discipline required, just recognizing the uniqueness of each person effectively.

Some people are just more motivated or more talented than others. You need to push some people, and you need to control others. I would much rather hold someone back a little who may be overly aggressive in their work habits than have to push a less motivated individual. Restraining an aggressive individual is easier and more productive, because it takes more time and effort to push. However, there are times when one push is all that a good person needs. David McNally's book *Even Eagles Need a Push* explains it well by relating that baby eagles are reluctant to leave the nest. All they need is a gentle push to get them out of the nest, and then they fly. Push and get out of the way.

Leaders who believe in the worth of the individual and mindfully lead with that value tend to be better leaders. Their organizations are more successful because their people are more than just numbers on the books. Having the right combination of people, talent, and skills all placed in a valued team environment is a major factor in successful organizations. Achieving that will be facilitated by managing each person according to their individual traits and skill level. When needed, productivity can be improved by tailoring the management approach to meet their performance needs.

Knowing and understanding what employees care most about is something often talked and written about. The lists of what employees value most is plentiful, and they are interestingly similar, but not all are the same. My personal belief is the two most important things people care about are trust and value. If leaders trust their employees, it allows the employee to earn a sense of pride, and that trust makes them feel they are important to the organization. The feeling of being a trusted worker creates personal value, which becomes exhibited in their efforts. When the boss cares about what you do, you will try harder.

There is no question that money will be a factor on the employees' care list, and in recent surveys, it was number one 55 percent of the time. That number clearly says there are other important considerations on their value list higher than money. A 2022 survey showed: a four-day work week, clean offices, fellowship, free time/work-life balance, recognition, learning and development, culture, meaningful work, and diversity. All of those issues were high on the list. Obviously, the newer survey differs from those lists of years ago.

However, my feeling remains that in dealing with people, trust is so important that it needs to be the cornerstone of any organization and any good leadership style. This is a significant part of the culture issue. If you are not a trusting leader, it will be more difficult for you and the company to meet your goals, the people's goals, and those of the organization. There have been books written about the impor-

*If you are not a trusting leader, it will be more difficult for you and the company to meet your goals, the people's goals, and those of the organization.*

tance of trust to the overall performance and success of companies. One I like is *The Speed of Trust* by Stephen Covey. It emphasizes that if you demonstrate trust in the person, it creates both personal value and a sense of well-being for the individual. Strong companies are the ones that value their people and put people first in the organizational culture. "My leader trusts me; therefore I have value here."

As a leader of people in any size environment, you should understand that people need to believe in you before they will believe in what you say. Until they have that belief, they are hesitant to accept what you are conveying to them. So, in a sense, you have a selling job to do about yourself with your people.

Ken Blanchard and Spencer Johnson's book *The One Minute Manager* stressed the timely acknowledgment of a job well done, because praise creates self-value, and has a strong impact on a person's attitude. Blanchard said not to miss the opportunity for praise. People love it, and you cannot say "thank you" too many times. Here is the recognition factor from the new survey: if "thank you" is done publicly, others on the team notice. So, recognition goes a long way toward having that all-important positive attitude, positive work environment, and personal satisfaction.

# CHAPTER 18

## RETAINING HEROES

*Embrace your heroes.*

In his leadership, my dad was concerned about any one person, or persons, becoming more important to the customer than the company was. I held a somewhat different view in that I liked having or creating heroes, no matter their position in the company. Obviously, there are going to be times when you are going to lose good people, and some of those may be your heroes. The better your company and the better the people are, the greater the chances of some being recruited away by other organizations. We are good at what we do and we have great people, so they are going to have offers, not all of which will turn out to be good opportunities for them. In one way, competitive recruiting comes with the risk of being good. But, realistically, would you want it any other way? You want your people to be an important and valuable resource to your customers—heroes! As important as they are, you cannot rely solely on your MVPs. Success is achieved by a total team effort, and the strengths, skills, and know-how of all the team members determine what you will be able to achieve.

In some of our company-wide gatherings, I pointed out our mobile service techs as a hero team, because when equipment was down, they showed up promptly to get it going again. They were instantly a hero to the customer.

Retaining good people is something that requires close attention by leaders and managers. If you are going to be consistently good, keeping your team together is high on the list of importance. If the company is strong enough, it's more important to customers than any one individual who left. That is to say, the company would survive the loss of the individual—even a hero. While that is true, no one likes to lose heroes, and while we have lost a few, I like the strong contribution heroes bring to the organization. Those individuals are heroes because they become very important to the customer. And, yes, there are plenty of internal heroes as well, because of the value they create and have to the company. Retention of people and heroes means your organization must be respected as the place where they want to be, where they are valued, and where they make a contribution.

We had a service manager who became a strong resource for our customers and was recruited away by one of our competitors who made many big promises to him. Dad was worried that many of our customers were going to leave us and go with him. I agreed that some might go, but our company was stronger than either that manager or the competitor. A few customers moved with the manager, but after two years of failed promises at that competitor and fewer resources to work with, both the manager and the customers were back with us. If a person chooses to leave, I encourage them to be very sure it will be better for them, as well as their family. You strive to prevent anyone making a lateral move. We do not want them to leave, but we are still going to be successful without them. The grass is not always greener on the other side of the fence; sometimes it's brown. I love having heroes, but I really hate to lose them.

We are very conscientious about providing personal employee value in the work environment and taking care of all—not just the heroes. There is no favoritism; rather, we exhibit fairness, caring, and trust to everyone. Over the years, we have had some people leave, and then want to come back. In a few cases, there was a place for them; but with many, their job had been filled. It was, in a way, a compliment to our company that they wanted to come back, but it's not always possible.

# Part Four
# Sales

# CHAPTER 19

## PERSONAL SALES SKILLS

*Sales is both fun and challenging.*

Each person in a sales role develops their own methods in their approach to the customer. There is no one right way to build sales skills. In today's world, data-driven sales methods are prominent, and how to interpret and use the information generated is critical to the success achieved. Many salespeople and managers are spending a lot of time learning how to turn data into a competitive advantage. Sales training opportunities and media materials are readily available and worth pursuing to develop and improve selling skills. Further, customers are different, and sales techniques can be individualized to fit a particular situation and customer. Having said that, there are some basic skills and knowledge involved in sales that help representatives and companies be successful.

After six years as a sales representative, I moved into the sales manager role, and it was a learning curve for me. I had many ideas formed from my selling experience, and I employed a number of those. I did a great deal of learning from as many sources and mentors as I could find. I spoke with and corresponded frequently with other sales managers I respected to learn, and use, many of their skills and methods.

## CHAPTER 20

## MAKING SALES A PART OF OUR CUSTOMERS' SUCCESS

*Be relevant in your customers' success.*

At STI, our strategy was to become successful by helping our customers be successful. When the customer asks, "How much do you know about my business?" we can say, "A lot—we can help you be better because our experience and products allow us to understand your objectives and desired outcomes." Being a trusted resource— possibly the most trusted resource and most valued partner—is a difficult and time-consuming task to accomplish. To achieve those goals requires building strong long-term, codependent relationships with customers. Being the most trusted resource to a customer is a very strong advantage if the opportunity is there to establish it.

It is very hard to be the leader in the marketplace when all competitors, as well as products, are basically equal. That is what is termed a commodity market. In a mature products industry with an established competitive environment, some change improvements simply do not generate greater profits. However, in efforts to move ahead of the competition, it is imperative that you create capabilities, benefits, and solutions that are valuable beyond the product in the customer's viewpoint. In other words, you need to offer something your competitors do not, or at the very least, be better than the competi-

*You need to offer something your competitors do not, or at the very least, be better than the competition at what you do offer.*

tion at what you do offer. You are looking for leverage to give you an advantage to increase the chances of winning. If you have a differentiation story, then you need to tell it, and tell it often, because offering something unique can be important to the buyer. This is especially true when any differentiation is directly relative to things that mean the most to customers. Additionally, if you can prove you have consistently delivered value with customer satisfaction, commitment, and performance, then you can use the proven consistency as a value differentiator. Regardless, you need a differentiated, value-added strategy if you are going to maximize your potential and be successful in a virtually equal competitive environment.

Developing those added values requires thoughtful sales planning around the targeted market. In my experience communicating with other companies, I have seen their plans fail because their plans were no more than just that—plans. Somehow the plans get relegated to the shelf and remain there. The team can sit around and talk about plans all day, but to be successful, someone must be responsible for coupling the ideas with actions, or nothing will happen. That is where good sales management comes into play to move the plans to life. Delivering the most value to customers depends on the consistency of executing your plans to the market.

---

*Being an information resource on trends, developments, how to, innovation, and other issues can become as meaningful to the customer as the monetary value of the product*

---

Customers determine the implicit value, not the one making the offer. The customer is setting the value based on what their needs are to be successful, what matters most to them, and who is providing the greatest value to them. How much value is contributed, how soon the value adds will begin, and how much confidence there is in the vendor's deliverability of the demanded values—all are included in the buying decision. Value adds are not only products or services, there are many ways to add value, and time spent determining them is important work. Information of all types is a powerful added-value tool to share with the customer. Information is the key to holding everything together and making things work. Today, we operate in an information-rich world, which only increases the requirement to be a resource in that space. In some instances, being an information resource on trends, developments, how to, innovation, and other issues can become as meaningful to the customer as the monetary value of the product. Competitively, the one who is setting the standards for the deliverability of his demanded values is where the customer will generally go as the first source.

# Some Things Don't Change

A long time ago, I read that there were three kinds of value: the kind the customer is willing to pay for; the kind the customer wants, but is not willing to pay for; and the kind the customer perceives has no value. Understanding customers' thinking on the value list is obviously critical in any proposal offered to them. What are the things the customer values most, and what are their expectations associated with each value?

# Chapter 21

## Remembering the Standard

*Your organization will be judged not only in comparison with your immediate competitors, but also by every place, person, and organization in which your customers, and others, come in contact with.*

Customer satisfaction is the front line of measurement of your company by everyone. The satisfaction level they received from every place where they have experiences—from customer service to purchases—will develop their expectations. It does not matter if a source of customer experience is not in your industry, what matters

---

*The satisfaction level they received from every place where they have experiences—from customer service to purchases—will develop their expectations. It does not matter if a source of customer experience is not in your industry, what matters is the best experience they receive from **any** source.*

---

is the best experience they receive from *any* source. That is the standard they remember—and customers will use those experience levels to judge their experience with your organization as well. For years the customer experience from Nordstrom was touted to be the measuring stick for everyone else—it did not matter that you were not in Nordstrom's industry. The more the story was told, the bigger it became. Creating outstanding customer experiences is what it is all about. Therefore, each and every interaction your company has with anyone will be a judgment on your company's performance. It is not only the sales representative's contacts, it is every time any person deals with anyone in your organization. Those interactions become a selling opportunity for the reputation of the company. Theoretically then, everyone in the company is in sales for the company. Up and down the organization, everyone needs to be creating good experiences in all contacts, no matter the reason; that is the objective.

For instance, we had a driver who drove one of our flat-bed trucks to deliver purchased equipment. One of our valued customers called to tell me the driver was one of the reasons he purchased from our company. The driver's attitude was always positive, he enjoyed his job, and he went over and above to ensure the delivery went well for the customer. When he unloaded the equipment, he cleaned it, made sure it ran well, and thanked the customer for doing business with us. He helped create a great customer experience! Earlier I referenced the importance of attitude, and this driver's behavior was good every day, no matter how long or hard he worked.

McDonald's was a game changer in the food service industry because they gave you a hamburger, fries, and a drink within minutes. Their innovation set a standard for customer expectations and helped fuel the desire for instant gratification, even if you were not buying hamburgers from McDonald's. To a great extent, we are living in a time where instant gratification is available from many sources—and we are doing business on McDonald's time, so to speak.

We all know about changing the game, or tilting the playing field in your favor, but it is exceptionally hard to do. When you ask yourself what you will do to differentiate yourself from your competitors, you need to be forward thinking, plan your strategy, and look for opportunities, products, people, and execution standards. These are just some of the ingredients leaders use in developing a value strategy. A CEO and good friend said that what you are trying to do is make 1 + 1 = 3 to add more value to the equation.

There will always be demand for the best, no matter the product, service, or industry. Being the best is the goal to set for your organization. It should be the outcome you pursue, because if you do not pursue it, you will not achieve it. You have to go for it! Remember, not only are you seeking new customers to add to your base, your overriding sales objective, as always, means that retaining the customers you have is integral to the plan.

# CHAPTER 22

## THINKING LIKE YOUR CUSTOMER

*Put yourself in the customer's shoes.*

You have to meet the customer where they are—in their space, in their mind, with their goals. Remember, it is not what you think the customer's values are, it is what the customer thinks their values are. So, what is he or she thinking? You may have the best product; however, in the customer's mind, product alone is not always enough. This is especially true with your more discerning customers who are just more demanding than others. A significant part of increasing customer expectations comes from things such as a more competitive market, better product quality, innovation, better fulfillment delivery, improved customer service, and the internet. Without a doubt, it is more of a challenge today than ever before to meet a customer's significantly increased expectations. Those expectations are driven by those components, which result in more added-value in the customer's buying experience.

Understanding the customer's values and requirements beyond the product itself will often be more important than just the product. If

---

*If you do a good job with discovery, you should know what the customer's issues or problems are that he or she needs to solve. Customers' values can change based on their current needs, and what is available to them. The ability to anticipate those changes in customer interest is very important to continued success.*

---

you do a good job with discovery, you should know what the customer's issues or problems are that he or she needs to solve. Customers' values can change based on their current needs, and what is available to them. The ability to anticipate those changes in customer interest is very important to continued success. I like to know the desired outcomes. "What outcome are you looking for?" It is a purpose-process-response method. If you know the purpose of the customer's intended needs purchase, your response can more effectively meet their requirements. What is the customer trying to accomplish that you can help and offer a solution? Purpose-response can be applicable in many circumstances, because once you have the appropriate information, you can do the necessary things to achieve the outcome.

In your sales presentation, try to present a story or proposal that solves the customer's issues, which will involve their participation in your proposal and solutions to achieve their goals. It becomes, "If we do this together, the outcome will solve your needs." Often, you can identify and feature what the customer's "wins" will be in the plan—and what will be the losses if the buyer goes in a different direction. The buyer must understand what the proposal does for him, so it needs to sound familiar to him. It needs to be communicated in an understandable way that does not feel threatening to achieve his goals. You need to talk in the way the customer thinks. Clarity in communications and presentations will breed curiosity in the customer's mind, and capture all complex issues and present an understandable proposal.

Emotions can play a role in buying decisions, and influencing the buyer's emotions will effectively help the decision process. Perhaps you can elicit a "We are missing out" or "I have to have that" reaction to your offer. Most all golfers react with "I have to have that" whenever a new driver hits the market. Car buffs react similarly to new or classic cars. Creating and using emotions fits well in the overall objective of generating a great buying experience for the customer. Telling stories of others' success with the product or idea can help generate the emotional factor.

---

*In your sales presentation, try to present a story or proposal that solves the customer's issues, which will involve their participation in your proposal and solutions to achieve their goals.*

---

I am sure we all have seen companies and people who do not go to the effort of, or do a poor job of, understanding what customers perceive to be their most important values. They are leaving money on the table, as the saying goes. In the discovery process, not only do you need to ask the buyer enough value questions, you need to make an effort to understand what the customer's overall big-picture objectives are. How does what the customer is doing now relate to his or her long-term goals, needs, and objectives? How do customers feel about where they are—satisfied or not—and what do they need to accom-

*In discovery, you need to ask, listen, and understand! This is especially true if it is a customer who is not currently buying from you. You need to know why they are not, and asking the right discovery questions can reveal why. The customer's answers can provide a wealth of useful information. Then, your solutions need to be focused on values within the customer-defined domain.*

plish their goals? In discovery, you need to ask, listen, and understand! This is especially true if it is a customer who is not currently buying from you. You need to know why they are not, and asking the right discovery questions can reveal why. The customer's answers can provide a wealth of useful information. Then, your solutions need to be focused on values within the customer-defined domain.

Apply this to your daily life as well because the more questions you ask, the more you learn.

This tactic goes back to remembering to listen. If you are the one doing all the talking, then you are not learning anything because you are not listening. We had a sales rep who talked so much he could talk himself into a sale and out of a sale in the same conversation. Making sales calls with him, I watched him talk so much that his message almost became irrelevant. I did my best to counsel him about some of the proper techniques of selling, but sadly, I had to bring him inside to telephone sales, effectively recasting him where he was more suited for the job. No matter the situation, being overly verbal (talking too much) does not add value to the content; as a matter of fact, it diminishes the value of the conversation.

During the discovery process, you may find one of the customer's values on which he or she places more importance than others. In their mind, there may be some absolutes that have to be met, such as on-time product delivery, quality, service, cost, product features, or something else entirely. Is there a make-or-break issue? If there is such a thing, then obviously you need to know that information. The primary or dominant dimension of the customer's values will be an important discovery, because you may or may not be the one who can offer the best value in that category. And you must know how you stack up against your competitors in each of the value dimensions— where you lead and where you fall short. Furthermore, are there any values you can deliver that the customer will perceive as unmatched? If there is a place where you have a clear competitive advantage, it may be possible for that advantage to overcome places where you fall short. However, if there are competitive absolutes either way, that information has to be determined. It simply cannot go unknown.

# CHAPTER 23

## THINKING COMPETITIVELY

*As you must think like your customer, you also
need to think like your competition.*

Remember, the competition is not dumb. If your competition is doing something well, that does not mean you should not do whatever is allowing them to be successful. In fact, it could mean you should be doing it as well, particularly if they are winning. Yet, just replicating will not be enough; it just becomes an inclusion to your offer. If you choose to have the same offering, look for ways to do it better than the current competitive method, because doing it the same way may not be as successful as you would like. Differentiation wins over replication every time. In creating your proposal, think: How can we execute this differently, or even create something that will be difficult to duplicate? The bottom line: it is much better to be a market creator, or leader, rather than a market sharer.

You should not lull yourself into thinking the competition won't do something you would not do, because it is likely they can, and will.

*Differentiation wins over replication.*

That kind of inside-the-box thinking can catch you unprepared. There are two things you should never undervalue or underestimate. First: do not undervalue what you have. Undervaluing your capabilities can lead to not seeing the opportunities that exist, as well as not maximizing your strengths to be competitive in the market. The second: never underestimate the competition.

Restricted thinking is analogous to situations when takeovers happen to companies. Takeovers are often precipitated by management failing to see the bigger picture of the opportunities that are available. Or perhaps they see them, but for some reason do not take advantage of them. That could be termed a narrow-minded vision by management. However, I do think if a company is on the lower range of performance, the opportunities available to them will then be on a lower scale. Sometimes companies operate in their own little space and never change. Being on autopilot makes it difficult to see the things that are not working as well as they should. To dig your way out of that hole, you have to pursue opportunities and changes that will generate greater success for the organization. Paragraph (limited) thinking in those situations will not be enough. The way out could mean finding a new path or building a new version of the organization. That engages the ability to also create more constructively within. Smart companies see a bigger space, a larger vision, and they are willing to take the risk to invest in new opportunities. With a takeover, the acquiring company sees the opportunities and is willing to take advantage of them. The acquiring company generally does well because of their ability to envision the way forward. They may or may not be thinking out of the box—they may not even have a box (limited vision).

I absolutely was not happy when our primary competitor caught us off guard—something that did not happen often—by doing something that we did not even imagine they would do. Years ago, there was no leasing of the type of equipment sold in our industry. A relative newcomer introduced leasing in their sales offers. It worked, and they were taking significant sales away from us. We had to scramble to meet the new buying options or risk continued sales losses. Were we caught off guard? Yes, as they changed the rules of the game and tilted the playing field to their advantage. A timely reaction by us and coordination with our supplier kept us in the game. Now most of our products are sold through lease packages. Do your very best to not allow the competition to get a one-up, because whoever can do something that the competition cannot do is one up on everyone else. It leaves the other parties playing defense and catchup, which is not a good position to be in. The "not invented here" rule can be limiting to your vision, so don't get caught up in that kind of thinking. It is not a good strategy, and can severely narrow your competitive options. Research, innovation, new ideas, and product development and improvement are winning strategies. Innovations drive growth and innovations require investment.

# CHAPTER 24

## MAKING FAST INNOVATIONS

*The need for speed.*

In today's fast-paced work environment, many companies are competing as if they are ahead of the game. Even if you are achieving success, you cannot let that success lead to complacency. The speed of change everywhere has accelerated, and in all likelihood will continue to move at a fast pace. If you are going to move faster, the entire organization must be aligned to do so in order to accomplish that goal. You need to know if and when the time is right for the organization to move at an enhanced pace. It is not about taking shortcuts or making mistakes, and it needs to be addressed with purposeful efforts. Often the need can be a reaction to market demands, which generates increased customer expectations. We have seen that mutual growth in an industry can be sped up by the degree of intensity from both existing and emerging competition. New competitors often bring new ideas and methods, which in some cases will mean do or die for existing companies to maintain their position. A need for a fast-paced change to compete will generally involve some risk-taking in order to maintain or improve your status in the industry. Any risks will need to be well thought through in order to avoid mistakes or digging a hole, which will be difficult to overcome. If the entire industry is moving forward fast, you must move with it or fall by the wayside.

Our company faced that environment in the 1990s when the golf industry grew at an unprecedented pace. For most of the nineties, golf course construction was in a high-growth mode. Courses were being constructed around the United States and the world in significant numbers. Competitively, we found we needed to be faster with our decisions, changes, and commitments than we had planned. That type of challenge may feel a little uncomfortable at times, but in a growth mode it will keep you with, or maybe even ahead of, the competition.

We did not need to think too long to understand that we either had invest in people and capabilities to grow with the trend or get out of the way and let someone else grow with it. Additionally, we could not accept the mindset of "We are as good as our competitors" and remain where we were. That is simply not a winning or successful formula. Comments like those came from a few other distributors in our industry who did not choose to grow with the industry. Soon enough, some were no longer around. We had to innovate and bring our A game in the growth and expansion, because competition, as well as new opportunities, demand you do so. We had to establish the competitive model and the processes, which enabled us to do better than others to achieve future success in the growth environment. Dean Smith said, "Don't take the shot your competitor wants you to take. Take the shot you want to take."

Many of the competitive elements of success are common; it is putting them all together that makes it work. The analogy would be like making a cake; if all the ingredients are used, then the cake will be good. If some are missing, or are not good ingredients, then the cake will not be as good as it could be. In most industries, the competitive environment today has become stronger and more intense than ever before. Around the globe, today's competition is highly capable, pushing all to use every resource they have in their arsenal to maintain position. People, products, innovation, execution, and brand components are contributing factors to sustainability. The strategy must be: What results do you want, and how do you make them happen—*timely*!

## CHAPTER 25

## DEFINE YOUR BRAND

*A brand is a communication about the*
*attributes of a company or product.*

Fostering a compelling reason for the customer to purchase your product is aided by developing and communicating a corporate theme or brand. Selling the brand is an important part of the presentation, but it is by no means all there is to it. That brand can be thematic, such as quality, service, innovation, product, history, or some combination of those. Brand identity can certainly convey the customer experience in its message. In each story category, you need to meet or exceed the customer's expectations to enhance the brand validity. You are communicating what you want to be believed about your organization, product, and services. What promise are you making, and in what way does your brand relate to your products and services? Is one or the other more important? If you can establish that brand theme, or belief, it becomes synonymous with your organization. The proposition becomes part of who you are—recognizable and established.

In our reorganization, we set outstanding customer service and best-quality products as central to our company's brand. Based on this identity, our company has remained true to that credence. Additionally, integrity and reliability are recognized by our customers as integral to our brand identity. A significant part of what makes a company strong is the position it owns in the mind of the customer. Establishment of a strong brand identity can enrich that belief.

The brand story can be developed around understanding the target audience. It must clearly include the purpose of the company and the benefits of the product. It is a story that should be short and simple for people to remember. Mercedes Benz has quality, McDonald's has fast service, Nordstrom has customer care. These are basic foundations of the company and are long-lasting values. The brand story can possibly contain your history or your future. If there is a wow factor to be had, and you can be the one to communicate and establish it, then the wow factor can be helpful in putting you over and above others by demonstrating, "This is us, who we are."

*If there is any one thing to which customers will be loyal, it is value.*

If there is any one thing to which customers will be loyal, it is value. The value issue is exactly where to put your best brand efforts and resources in play. In our case, we delivered the best product, supported by the best after-sale support, by the most knowledgeable representatives. In other words, the value was in the *total* package, which would be very difficult for the competition to duplicate. Over time, those criteria worked their way into our brand recognition. I have often thought our brand proposition had become a bit too broad, but it evolved over years, and is verified by our customer comments. History proves there will always be a need for the best, as judged by the customer.

# CHAPTER 26

## THE LOW-PRICE PROVIDER

*No matter what you do, some customers*
*are going to try a low-cost provider.*

There are customers who will always be driven by cost. Even given that, there remain many decision factors in the customer's bucket, beyond the product itself. If you are not going to be the price leader, then the task is to give them compelling reasons *not* to go in the price-only direction. To compete against the price-only firms, much of the customer's mindset needs to be known and addressed. Generally speaking, low-price providers tend to have gaps in their offer (from products to service) that can be revealed with enough work in the discovery process. Those are most often easy to determine, and the idea is to use those reasons to your advantage. There are underlying reasons someone can be a low-cost provider and that strategy will contain limits in their value proposition, such as innovation, quality, and service. Generally, low-cost providers need higher volume to maintain their business, and if volume dissipates, they begin to suffer. Additionally, low-price offerings can put stress on the profit margins associated with commodity-type products.

The more a market moves toward a commodity environment, the more important it becomes to have and use your value-added abilities.

# CHAPTER 27

## BEING CONSISTENT

*Understand the importance of undeviating.*

Being consistent means doing things the same way over time in order for it to become believable, reliable, and therefore successful. It is a long-term commitment you make and is a driver of success. Consistency is a journey, not an event. If done well to a high standard, it will become integrated in the recognizable brand component of the company. Consistent performance builds trust for the organization, and you could very well say it is the biggest contributor to being successful. No matter what you do or how you do it, if the delivery is not consistent, success falls through the cracks.

There are a number of reasons for inconsistent performance in companies. Some causes are due to the quality of people changing, opportunities fading, products changing, or monetary issues. Also, leaders may fail to pay close attention to changing circumstances. You cannot take your eye off the ball, as they say. Discipline is required to maintain consistency in all areas and in every action taken by the organization. For any organization to be great, it must have discipline in adhering to the established performance standards and methods over time. They will not achieve long-term success without it, because it is the performance to expected standards over a long period of time that makes it a reality. This cannot be a short-term measurement; it is an ongoing adherence to excellence in execution. The standards set and expected are the framework for the discipline required to drive consistent results.

Consistency means that the best people focus on and perform the tasks required to produce the desired results every day. You have to follow the plan, meaning the effort to do so cannot come and go. It is a difficult challenge to maintain top-level performance and requires leaders, managers, and team members to have constant eyes on those tasks. You must know what the right things are that will determine consistent success, or it will not happen. Consistency is not always just the big things; it is knowing and doing things—both big and small—well, over and over again. It is doing the hard things well, not just the easy ones. Yes, there are some functions that are critical success factors, and those require more attention, but everything counts in consistency. A culture of consistency is grounded in the attention to detail, and I firmly believe the commitment to that

*There are not a lot of tasks more important than consistency of execution in the success of any organization.*

scrutiny is driven from the top.

This may sound simple, but it is not; it takes a considerable amount of work, determination, and attention to make it work. Inconsistency of efforts leads to low performance, mediocrity, or even unsuccessful companies. There are not a lot of tasks more important than consistency of execution in the success of any organization.

A member of the UNC golf team said, when he was told by his coach to get ready for a match, "If I stay ready, then I don't have to get ready." Mario Cristobol, football coach of the University of Miami Hurricanes, said it well, "Don't practice until you get it right, practice until you can't get it wrong." Which is possibly another way of saying: practice what makes you better.

---

*Consistency of performance is earned, not a given from the start, and is accomplished by the discipline to stick to principles, no matter the current environment faced.*

---

Consistency of performance is earned, not a given from the start, and is accomplished by the discipline to stick to principles, no matter the current environment faced. There is little doubt that consistency over time has been a strong contributor to the success our company has achieved. Being consistent is not a once-in-a-while thing—it has to happen every day, from top to bottom, for years and years.

# CHAPTER 28

## RECOVERING FROM YOUR FAILURES

*Customers will hold you to your promised performance and are reluctant to forgive you for not meeting your commitments.*

Surveys indicate that 91 percent of customers who complain about failed service do not come back. If a failure occurs, the recovery process must be exceptionally good, or even beyond what is acceptable, in the customer's mind. Those same surveys show 95 percent of customers will come back if the recovery process meets or exceeds their expectations. It is even possible that a well-handled recovery can create more loyalty than was enjoyed before the failure. It creates a "we have

*Surveys indicate that 91 percent of customers who complain about failed service do not come back.*

your back if something goes wrong" belief.

When doing recovery, I used to ask the customer, "What would you like for us to do?" While this is not a unique question, most of the time it opened up a starting point and allowed me to understand where the customer's thinking was. Sometimes, their wants were more than we could provide. However, I was often surprised about how little it took to make a disgruntled customer happy just by making the effort to do so. In recovery, if the customer is emotionally upset you cannot get anywhere maintaining the same attitude in your response. That will just increase the intensity of the conversation. You cannot bully a bully, as that will get you nowhere, and only lead to a stalemate or even a failed recovery. When communicating in most any situation, do not raise your voice, because the moment you do that, the other person stops listening. You just lost! The person tunes you out, and their concentration moves away from what you are saying to the level of your voice. The better way is to show some understanding and agreement with their issue, such as, "I would not like it if that happened to me either." That response shows empathy and understanding of their mindset; it puts you on their level and calms their emotions.

---

*The majority of the time, the customer does not care how the failure happened; they only want to know what you are going to do for them. The sooner you can tell them you are going to take care of their issue and how you are going to do it, the better the outcome will be.*

---

You cannot always do what the customer is asking for, of course, because in the heat of the moment those expectations tend to be somewhat elevated. Customers are not always right, they are wrong frequently. However, you do need to acknowledge and take responsibility for a failure, rather than attempt to make excuses for the occurrence. The majority of the time, the customer does not care how the failure happened; they only want to know what you are going to do for them. The sooner you can tell them you are going to take care of their issue and how you are going to do it, the better the outcome will be.

Performance failures need to be taken seriously and not allowed to fall through the cracks. That is absolutely the worst thing to have happen in a failure occurrence. Tracking and monitoring the recovery effort need to be someone's specific responsibility and the response monitoring should happen without letting much time go by. A follow-up should be made to the customer to ensure their satisfaction. Sometimes, but not always, you can come out as a hero through really well-executed recovery efforts. Again, the thing you do not want to do is fail to make the recovery effort, because in the customer's mind, the failure to make that effort is another failure, and it will be the last nail in the coffin.

# CHAPTER 29

## PRODUCT SUPPORT EFFORTS

*After the product is delivered to the customer,*
*your required value to the customer goes up a notch.*

Our company has always believed high-level after-sale service support of our products has been a strong differentiator in our favor. For products that require post-purchase support, you have to be able meet the commitment of that service obligation. Customer satisfaction and retention demands that you meet the inherent after-market service responsibility. In addition, with delivery of the product, your value becomes incorporated into the product itself, because a significant amount of the buyer's expectations of product confidence are dependent on the ability of the seller to support the reliability of the product. If after-market support is required and you are not adding that value to the transaction, then you clearly have a shortcoming in your importance, and value, to the customer.

# Some Things Don't Change

Failure to meet the support needs of the customer can transition into the loss of future business with the customer. We all have seen buyers leaving a product or vendor because of failures in after-purchase support. Frequently, the two most important components of after-sale support in an industry like ours are repair and replacement parts. For customer satisfaction and retention, both of those obligations have to be met on a timely basis.

A big plus is that when customers are receiving good support in their current relationship, they are less likely to go to another product or supplier. In our years of giving product support, we have had feedback from customers who tell us they buy where they get the best service. Thankfully, that has been us, because we made customer support in all areas a priority.

In product support instances, after-market service can become the customer's most important required value. A valued customer of ours was working with a golf course architect on a new course construction. The architect was promoting a particular product company to the customer because he was receiving compensation to do so. After several discussions about this, the customer said, "I need to tell you something to resolve this issue. I buy my equipment where I get the best service, and around here, that is Smith Turf and Toro, so that is where I will purchase my equipment. I do not want to this to come up again."

After-sale product support is a value category of its own because of the importance surrounding it and the many ways to provide that service support. There is nothing new about required product support; the magic is in making it happen—to the customer's satisfaction!

# CHAPTER 30

## STAND BEHIND YOUR SALES REPS

*Those who represent the company play a big part in the value that is significant to the customer.*

Before I talk about the traditional role of sales representatives, let's address some important developments taking place. Technology and the advent of online buying has moved the sales function further away from in-person selling in many situations. The movement is changing the sales structures of organizations in a number of ways, and will continue to do so going forward. The inside sales staff are taking on more and more responsibility in the overall sales as they increasingly become the first point of contact for customers. However, that trend is not true in all organizations and the outside sales people will retain their importance to the company and the customer. That said, let's talk about the sales representatives.

The client-customer relationship and the customer's ability to interact directly with a sales representative can become very high on the customer's list of values. Representatives have the ability to convey much more than just product details to customers, and the better they are, the more resourceful they become to the customers. In a signifi-

People buy from people

cant way, people buy from people. If a representative is good, then he or she is selling himself or herself as well as the product and company.

It is vital for companies to stand behind their people and sales representatives in their dealings with customers. Companies need to have sales representatives' backs, and those representatives need to understand they have the company's support. Customers also need to know the company supports its representatives and the commitments they make on behalf of the company. If a representative makes a commitment to the customer, and the company vetoes the commitment, or fails to deliver it, then you will likely lose the customer as well. The organization's support for and trust in its people go a long way toward gaining the customers' support and confidence. It is more than just selling the product—it is creating value. Representatives are responsible for developing and maintaining good business relationships for the organization.

The relationships, which your representatives build with customers, can be a real competitive advantage—no doubt about it. Customers are looking for an "experience" with product, service, resource, and relationships. The sale differentiator can be the relationship and connection that your representatives build with the customer. Competitively, it becomes, "my guy can outsell your guy." Knowledgeable, articulate, and dependable representatives, who present themselves well to the customer, are essential to success. I am old school enough to believe that when a person steps in the customer's door, he or she should look successful, act successful, and be dependable. Perhaps a notch above the competition. Those are the ones to recruit and represent your organization. While some form of remote work is here to stay, as video has proven to be an effective way to communicate with customers, face time between sales reps and customers will retain its importance in building and maintaining strong customer relationships.

Communicate with your representatives often, for they are the ones face-to-face with the customer on the frontlines. They understand the customer's needs, the competition, and the market since they are the ones talking directly with your customers. Every conversation, friendship, common interest, or business your people have with a customer enriches the relationship for the company. Yet the more meaningful and resourceful the content of those conversations, the stronger the representative's value becomes. If reps are good enough and work to be a trusted resource for the customer, then they and the company have created an advantage over the competition.

Many companies understand that the more time spent in contact with the customer, the better the relationship becomes. Most leaders measure a larger part of success by the numbers, and that is not all bad; however, an equally important measurement is the relationships created with your customers by any means.

Sales people are not managing outcomes as much as they are coordinating the outcome with those who have other jobs like service, fulfillment, customer service, admin, and so forth. Representatives provide a single point of contact for the customer to facilitate the buying activities (experience), and they are primary in maintaining customer relationships. Do sales reps generate 100 percent of the sales? No, but their relationships not only create the original sale, they maintain the future sales opportunities. Personally, I give them a lot of credit for generating sales. The entire sales function of the company takes a coordinated team, and it requires a division of responsibilities among each of the workflow functions to effectively accomplish the sale. Sales managers are the ones who are charged with managing the overall sales workflow and the successful sales outcome. Our previous CFO liked to say, "A sale is not a sale until it is paid for; until then it is a delivery." When payment is delayed, it can require more than just the accounting people to be involved. Both the sales rep and the sales manager may need to assist in the collection efforts, even though they generally do not like to do so. That is divided responsibilities coming together to finalize the process.

The saying goes, "hindsight is 20/20," and as I look back over my career, I did not do a good job of spending time with our sales representatives making calls and talking with our customers. I think in terms of the value chain to the customer, there are many positives emanating from the CEO being face-to-face with the buyer. It is important, and often not easily accomplished, but I should have made the opportunity for that to happen more than I did.

When I first started as a sales rep, I was riding to a basketball game with a friend who owned his own company. He suggested a tool I might use: "Ask your customers for help with something. People naturally like to help other people, and if you ask them for their help, they will go out of their way to help you. It will help create a bond, they will feel good about helping someone, and it will let them know that you value their opinion." I used this tool many times, and it worked just as Jim had said. In addition, I also learned a lot by listening to their input, as well as things they needed help with. It was a two-way exchange. There are probably other circumstances and ways in which this tool can be beneficial as well.

I once told our major supplier that with every step or level you are away from the customer, it becomes easier to make poor customer-oriented decisions. I still believe that. And I say all this while knowing the impact the internet has had on the customer and in the buying cycle. The go-to-market structure is not the same everywhere, so the sales strategy is not all the same. It is the effective implementation of the "how to" in the sales strategy that is paramount. The better you know the intended customer, the more successful you are!

# CHAPTER 31

## ENSURING COMPETITIVE ADVANTAGES

*Outperform your competitors.*

A sustainable advantage is an attribute that allows an organization to outperform its competitors over time. That advantage, if it is real, can be part of the go-to-market planning and strategy. You hear a lot about a sustainable advantage, and that is certainly achievable in some cases, but I think in today's world it is limited to fewer organizations, and perhaps is becoming almost obsolete in achievability. From information to resources, from R&D to manufacturing, it is very difficult to create and hold a unique competitive advantage for a long period of time. Some form of highly difficult-to-duplicate differentiation is the real key to the sustainable advantage door. It seems the more companies there are in a field, the fewer opportunities there are for sustainable advantages. Your product will continually have more challenges, and to maintain the advantage it will have to stand above products that will be very similar. Success breeds success; and why is that? Because the more successful you are, the more opportunities you are going to have to execute your offering. Effective competitiveness depends on how well a company organizes themselves around their tasks, people, capabilities, resources, and responsiveness. It is the sum of values, all of which need to be closely monitored and continually updated in order to be organizationally successful. Still, it is extremely difficult to create and maintain a sustainable competitive advantage.

Remember, a competitive advantage does not necessarily mean a sustainable advantage. A company or product may be able to create a unique advantage for a period of time, but most all do not translate to a long-term sustainable advantage. Sustainable advantages come from attributes like size, know-how, experience, marketing, innovation, vertical integration, and horizontal differentiation. There are companies and products that we all remember having what, at the time, looked to be a sustainable advantage that no longer have that: perhaps Coca-Cola at one time, Henry Ford's automobile, Blackberry, Kodak, AOL, and Motorola.

Competitively speaking, it is difficult to get to be king of the hill, but it is even more difficult to stay there. Years ago, our company was on top and winning awards in our industry. We are still winning awards, but not as many, even though our capabilities are as good or better than ever. What happened? Everybody else got better, including the competition. For a long time, I kept a piece of paper in my desk drawer so I could look at it frequently with two large printed notes on it: "Continued Improvement & Process Improvement." It was a visual reminder of "What can we do better?" It simply reinforces the understanding that you cannot sit still or coast. If you are not improving, you are essentially losing momentum, or perhaps even moving in reverse. Great organizations are the ones who keep moving forward. What changes have you made lately? You almost have to get ahead of yourself to take advantage of opportunities. Movement does not always translate into progress if capabilities are not matched to the changes.

---

*If you are not improving, you are essentially losing momentum, or perhaps even moving in reverse. Great organizations are the ones who keep moving forward. What changes have you made lately?*

---

At a meeting some time ago, the national sales manager and the president of one of our major national competitors came to me. They had been studying our company, and they were going to try to duplicate our company model for their distributors nationwide. They said, "If we can be you, we can beat anybody." I took that as great compliment, and I wished them well. Unfortunately for their company, neither of them stayed with their company long enough to achieve the goal. I was told later by one of their associates that they did not realize the resources, time, and cost it would take to establish what it took us years to achieve. That former company did not get better, and later moved out of the US market. Being consistently good over time is difficult, as they discovered. Today it is far more difficult to stay ahead of the game, keep up, or change ahead of or with the market. As a business objective, it takes great effort, vision, investment, and willingness. It is not easy to achieve a sustainable advantage. As Kermit the Frog would say, "It's not easy being green."

# CHAPTER 32

## MAKING THE BUSINESS SUSTAINABLE

*Create long-term business value.*

Sustainability means what we need to do to keep the business going in terms of sales revenues. But clearly, that simple statement involves so much more. Sustainability means planning and having all of the resources necessary to progress forward over time with continued success. It is how to be profitable and grow. Therefore it is all-encompassing, from leadership to people, to adding capabilities, to ideas, to innovation. It requires decisions, changes, investments, products, people, infrastructure, and shaping the organization to remain relevant in the future. Planning uses a great deal of data—financial and historical—to make decisions which surround sustainability because of the importance of the issue and the monetary impact included in creating forward value for the company.

Sustainability is in the deliverability of your product, services, and

189

customer focus against environmental, social, market, and governmental measures. It is just not an every-now-and-then thing, it is every day. It is the operational efficacies, economic issues, cost controls, and people required to create profitability. You have to be able to deliver in the good times as well as the difficult times. This planning and development must be instilled in every person throughout the entire organization for financial success to become a habit. Habits are powerful in most any endeavor. When you can get performance to be a high-level habit with reliable outcomes, you are on the road to forward success.

Sustainability is the long-term part of corporate strategy, and therefore requires long-term vision, objectives, and goals. Organizational sustainability planning considers what we currently have and what we need to obtain or eliminate in the future to provide value to all concerned and to sustain the business going forward. It is today's knowledge applied to future possibilities, because what you do now will control what you do later. So, start your sustainability planning and activities with the end in mind—where you want to be in the future. And, as the radio program title goes, "All Things Considered."

# CHAPTER 33

## BEING PROACTIVE

*Be proactive, not reactive, in your sales efforts.*

Accomplishing your sales objectives requires you to think about and anticipate the future in terms of needs or changes. It means you have to be willing to take the first step and look for opportunities for advancement or improvement. Being proactive provides the ability to stay ahead of the curve. To stay ahead, you must try to be smarter, more proactive, and more responsive than your competitor is. This is very difficult to achieve, and easier said than done.

Playing catchup, from product to services, leaves far too many missed opportunities on the table. Many companies operate reactively, and they are late to the game, forcing them to continually play catchup. In our industry, there were companies who waited for Toro (the innovative leader) to introduce new products. Then, as their strategy, they would try to duplicate them. Operating in a retroactive environment is never a good competitive strategy. It puts you in a follow-up mode to things that have already happened.

If a company operates with a proactive strategy, they are able to make decisions without being encumbered by attempting to respond to preexisting situations. You cannot always be proactive, but it helps to have that thinking in your planning. It also helps to take some of the risk out of future activities. Risks such as running out of money, customer care failures, or product failures. It will increase your chance of success and decrease chances of failure because of the preparation involved in the activity.

An example of being proactive came early in my role as sales manager. I determined we needed to add two sales representatives to our staff. Dad was more on the conservative side of leadership, and I tended to be more of a risk taker. My dad thought we needed to wait for the demand to build before we added to the sales staff because that was what he did. Dad was a good leader and the company was very successful. He was very highly respected in our industry, and Ed Seay, Arnold Palmer's design partner, once told me, "Your dad is the best person I have ever dealt with." This was a great compliment, because the Palmer organization worked with top people worldwide. Yet Dad's methods were just different from mine; he was less of a risk taker. I suggested that if we waited, it would take years for the demand to build. The market was changing and we needed to create the demand, not wait for it to build. Besides, if we did not act, our competition probably would, and we would then be in a catchup position for years. We needed to be proactive, not reactive. He relented and we added the two representatives. Being proactive requires constant adaptiveness to the needs of the customers. The additional reps proved to be the correct response to the market opportunity.

# CHAPTER 34

## YOU NEED TWO FOLLOWS

*Follow up and follow through.*

For a long time, I have been talking about the "two follows" with our sales team. These are *follow up* and *follow through*. To be completely honest, I never thought I should need to talk about these two issues with anyone. However, from time to time, instances came up that prompted me to speak with someone about the importance associated with these two skills. Similar to decisiveness and procrastination, these "two follows" are also related to each other.

It certainly is not difficult to understand the meaning of *follow up*. It is the execution of the principle that is the issue. The importance of effectively using follow-up cannot be overstated, and a failure to follow up can be devastating in many respects. It is a valued characteristic in all aspects of your life, both personal and professional.

A simple explanation: in the sales environment, if a sales representative told a customer, "I will get you a price on a product," and then failed to deliver that price, he would lose a great deal in the customer's perception. The customer would then see the sales representative as not dependable, honest, respectable, or trustworthy. It would be safe to assume the customer would look elsewhere, and the sale would be lost. Or perhaps in everyday life people say, "I will call you later"— then do not call. Follow-up is a commitment to act, and a failure to respond in a timely manner will definitely result in a loss of confidence in the individual who failed.

*Follow through*, on the other hand, refers to the second part of the commitment. It is a personal responsibility to see a task through to completion, which can be measured in terms of outcomes. *Following through* means you can't stop halfway through on the task. There are no medals for just a ninety-yard dash. Finish the responsibility associated with the commitment.

Both of the "follows" are critical personal skills that build trust and credibility between people at any level. Many people make promises with good intentions and then lack the motivation or responsibility to uphold the commitments. Respect and integrity are lost quickly when one fails in either of these areas. As a result, people believe you don't care enough about them or their issues. Follow-up and follow-through are doing what you said you would do, when you said you would do it, without exceptions.

# CHAPTER 35

## THE SALES TOP 10 LIST

Here is my top ten list of selling.

1. Return calls promptly.
2. Be on time.
3. Deliver what you promised, when you promised.
4. It's okay to say "I don't know" (if you follow it with "I will find the answer").
5. Follow up and follow through.
6. Listen to understand.
7. Be respectful.
8. Be honest.
9. Be professional.
10. Be aggressive—do a little more—go the extra mile.

# Technology: A Brief Comment

Technology has changed everything. The internet shapes and influences our daily lives and controls much of the world's economy. Technology is such an extensive and fast-moving topic that I am not going to attempt to go into the details of the subject. It will continue to impact our lives, both personal and business.

At a seminar during the infancy of the internet, I asked writer and consultant Tom Peters if there was a business or industry anywhere that would not be affected by the internet—to which he gave a strong no. It quickly became the standard, not an option, in all aspects of business and personal activities. These days you must have customer support, sales, products, knowledge/training on the use of products, and a lot more available to the customer online. It is not just that you have it, the application of online capabilities is what makes it work for you. It has to be user-friendly and comprehensive.

Digital workflow will continue to be transformational in the business environment. The information world has moved, and everything has moved with it. Work by paper has decreased, communication has transitioned, manufacturing is much advanced, buying is different and easier, and the list keeps going—improving. The digital world has also reduced face-to-face communication in many situations.

# Some Things Don't Change

With the internet, customers are also far more informed about products and services than ever. In many ways, with the knowledge available on the internet, the dynamics have changed. Technology allows the customer to be in charge—not the seller. Which means the internet has allowed business to become a buyer's market, rather than a seller's market. There are more and more examples of this movement, from the apparel market to car buying and many more to come. Often, with their online search capabilities, buyers know as much, or more, about your products as you do. The information is out there and readily available. No longer is there a significant competitive advantage in technology, because everyone has it, and it is simply a required tool in your kit. As we have seen, in many cases, the internet is solely where many businesses exist—no brick and mortar, no sales staff, just online. Year after year, a larger and larger percentage of business sales strategy and success is moving to a digital platform. It can be all of your go-to-market plans or part of them. Either way, digital is here.

What is presently happening is uncontrolled digital surveillance. The major technology companies are, in one way or another, tracking almost everything we do. In the business world, this provides them with a mountain of data, from which they are able to do targeted selling. It is predictive extraction, for which not enough adequate laws or standards are yet in place to govern those activities.

Artificial intelligence will be the most significant development man has ever created. It will be able to do wonderful things, and do them in a matter of seconds what could have taken decades for our best human minds to accomplish. AI is billions of times more powerful than human intelligence. It is projected to solve many of the ailments of the human body resulting in longer life spans, and so very much more on every front you can imagine. AI will automate or change a large majority of jobs and will replace some entirely. Many workflow jobs will be significantly enhanced by AI. Virtually every industry will be influenced by AI.

On the other side of the coin, the ease of fake information and the danger therein will be formidable and difficult to control, so there will need to be global rules and regulations for AI use. Elon Musk has emphasized the dangers of AI and is quoted as saying AI "has the potential of civilization destruction" and has expressed the need for control to the greatest extent possible. However, history would suggest that laws do not necessarily keep the bad guys from getting and using very harmful things. Perhaps the scariest concern of AI is completely automated weapons. Wars fought totally by machines with no human intervention and the machines making the decisions. From fake information, to war, to science, to manufacturing, the world will evolve in an entirely new way.

Hopefully, AI ethics will be in place soon enough, because projections of extreme misuse are prolific. Singularity will surely happen. Singularity is the moment when artificial intelligence forges ahead on its own at an uncontrollable pace and leaves its human creators behind. It will be intelligent enough to work around any on/off switch or other efforts of control. Over time, how do you control something that is more powerful than its creator?

# Conclusion

If you are still reading—thank you! There may be a number of things I did not talk about, or things you have differing opinions about, or even would have said in another way. That is okay. I understand. I was encouraged to speak and share my thoughts about four issues. There is much more extensive information out there, and I would encourage you to seek it out. Be curious and ask questions, listen, read, and watch. Learning never stops, and acquiring new understandings is self-improvement for all. I have enjoyed discussing these subjects and sharing my beliefs and insights. These are things I learned, used, and they worked for me. Some may work for you.

# ACKNOWLEDGMENTS

I would like to thank several people for their help with this endeavor. Thank you to Erica Messimer for the encouragement to go forward and to speak my thoughts. Thank you to Mac Alexander for his feedback.

Thank you to Betsy Thorpe, my editor, for your editing and all of your valuable advice. Thank you to Katherine Bartis for copyediting and proofreading, and Diana Wade for the book and cover design. This book is better because of all of you.

# THE SMITH LEGACY

## FOR YOUR INFORMATION

No. 16-L . . . May 16, 1945

### TRIBUTE TO A GOOD GUY

Attached you will find an illustration of a new Sales and Service Building that is going to be erected just as soon as materials become available, by Earl Smith of Charlotte, N.C.

The story of Earl Smith, if fully written by some competent writer, would be a combination of Lazarus, Horatio Alger, and Believe-it-or-not Ripley, all rolled into one -- and because it is not only interesting but stimulating reading, of how a man can come back after major reverses and make a success of an enter-prise -- it is well worth the pat on the back we are going to give him now.

Earl came with us in the spring of 1925 after taking a severe licking in the furniture business -- in fact about all he had left was a wife, two small boys, a Jewett automobile, and a few hundred dollars in cash.

When he came over to our plant to talk to us about selling machinery, we told him there was an opportunity in Florida, but that he would have to find the way himself because we had never sold anything in Florida and about all we could offer him was a few inquiries which had come in and he could have these to work on. Beyond that he would have to make his own way.

Finances were a bit difficult so we told him he could make a couple of stops on the way down and possibly pick up enough orders to pay his expenses, and keep going. With this meager start, away he went.

I remember vividly the day he left with his wife -- the two small boys suit cases and a few odds and ends wedged tight in the Jewett Car which was already well worn. There hardly seemed enough room left to put a few catalogs to show customers. And when he said goodby at the curb and drove off down the street, it made a lump rise in our throat. -- Here was a display of genuine courage.

He stopped at Memphis and sold one or two items -- stopped at Birmingham and did the same thing -- and then at Atlanta -- and finally he wound up in Jacksonville Florida, still intact.

The next few years changed the picture radically and he did a great job selling our machinery from one end of Florida to the other and developing a profitable business -- and along with it, a lot of prestige and goodwill for E. J. Smith.

This went along until the boom in Florida collapsed and got him on the wrong side of a number of real estate promotions in which he lost all of his money. To make matters worse he not only lost all he had -- but was heavily indebted to various companies, including ourselves.

To go broke once in a lifetime is enough -- but to go broke twice has floored many a man. But instead of giving up and calling quits -- this little one hundred and twenty-five pound giant again packed his wife and boys and the remnants of their furniture in a car and drove up to Charlotte and started all over again from the basement of a house. His only wealth the experience gained in Florida, he gradually accumulated sufficient friends and along with them sufficient business to move from the basement into a small building, while his two boys worked after school in filling stations to help out the family exchequer.

In recent years his business has expanded to where his annual volume is in excess of $250,000 per year -- his two boys have grown up and are partners with him in the business, and one is now a Lieutenant in the Navy.

Every cent of his obligations in the Florida crash have been paid off in full. He could have taken the easier course and wiped the slate clean in one sweep -- but he chose not to do so and instead determined to pay them off gradually, which he has done.

This new building is a living monument to a little guy with a bad leg, who neither smokes, drinks or swears -- but who has a soft voice and a pleasant smile which has caused one of his contemporaries in Atlanta to offer the comment that North Carolina is a Sahara for anybody else but Smith.

So we are glad to pay him this tribute, and feel that he fully deserves it.

Yours very truly,

K. E. Goit
Vice President

K.E.Goit-W

*Memo from Toro Vice President K.E. Goit, May 16, 1945.*

# GRIT!

By
T. S. HOOK

Courage isn't merely a quality one expects from men in battle. It's also a requirement in business, where sudden unforseen changes of the market may mean complete and total obliteration of years of labor and hard-earned savings. A man can perhaps weather one such set-back, but rare indeed is the man who can survive *two* complete failures to become successful.

In the spring of 1925, a young man of small stature suddenly found his foundation knocked from under him when the furniture business he had worked so hard to build collapsed, leaving him with a wife, two small boys, and a well-worn Jewett automobile—and no means of support. Recovering from the blow of fate, he found his way to Minneapolis and asked the Toro Company for a position selling their machinery. The mower manufacturer informed him that there was an opening in Florida, but it meant finding the way himself in virgin territory, for the company hadn't sold anything in that state. All the firm could do was to offer him a few inquiries that had come in.

Finances, too, were a problem, and the young man was told he would have to work his way to Florida by making a couple of stops here and there. It was a stiff challenge, but Earl J. Smith accepted without qualification.

A lump came to the throats of those who watched the old Jewett car leaving the Minneapolis factory. There was hardly room for a few catalogs for showing customers, so high was the auto piled with suitcases, the remnants of the Smith furniture, and the family of four. But the little man at the wheel had his chin high as he guided the worn car down the road and headed south.

At Memphis, the new garden equipment salesman sold a few items. In Birmingham and Atlanta, a few more —and finally the Smith family and their undaunted head arrived in Jacksonville, Florida, all in one piece.

The next few years gave E. J. Smith a profitable business, for people liked the soft-spoken man with the ready smile. The prestige and good will which grew for this little man promised even greater success. But success doesn't always come and stick with the most deserving—and when the Florida land boom went up it caught E. J. Smith on the wrong side of some real estate promotions—and hopelessly in debt.

But Earl had a wealth of experience from his Florida business, and he had learned from failure. One again he packed his family into his car, this time heading for Charlotte, North Carolina. There he began operations in the basement of a rented house. He soon made friends and customers, and his boys

worked in a nearby filling station to help with the family exchequer. He next moved into a small shop, and in 1946 opened the present Sale and Service Building distributing lawn and golf supplies for both Carolinas. At the opening he sponsored a golf tournament and barbecue, and thousands honored the plucky little man who had failed twice to come back and do a million dollar volume annually!

Today, E. J. Smith and Sons Co. occupies a two-story building on a property area of 300 by 125 feet, with forty-five employees, and they distribute for Toro Whirlwind and the Clinton Machine Co., in addition to handling Springfield Garden Tractors, Milorganite fertilizer Rotoette, Onan generators, and allied merchandise such as grass seeds, sprayers, spikers, and miscellaneous equipment relative to the industry.

The debts incurred in the Florida failure have been paid in full, and he and his sons have become an example of American courage. Laugh at failure —success can be around the corner, if you keep trying, says E. J. Smith.

*"GRIT!" was written by T.S. Hook and published by The Toro Company.*

# MEN OF ACHIEVEMENT
# IN THE CAROLINAS

## Earl Judson Smith . . . . CHARLOTTE, N. C.

Born in Stillwater, Minn., February 23, 1887. Married the late Irene Delmarse of Minneapolis, Minn. They have two sons, Wayne B., and George R. Smith, who are associated with their father in business. He later married Rubie Beam of Rutherfordton, N. C.

Mr. Smith is President and Treasurer of E. J. Smith and Sons which he originally organized in Jacksonville, Florida, in 1925 as a distributing company for turf maintenance equipment. He moved the business to Charlotte in 1933 and in 1936 added lines for distribution to all golf course professional shops. This company has the unique distinction of being the only distributors selling both golf course maintenance equipment of golf supplies through the golf professionals' stores. They cover the entire Southeast and serve 650 "pro" shops and golf courses. The company was incorporated in 1946 and has grown steadily each year since 1933.

Mr. Smith is well known to all golf professionals and has worked closely with the United States Golf Association. As a consequence he has drawn many professional golfers to Charlotte.

He is an Elder of the Avondale Presbyterian Church, a member of the Optimist Club and the Carmel Country Club and is also active in all civic and golf affairs.

This is a success story of a man who had an idea, secured merchandise which was in demand and stuck to the job of selling it until his customers looked to him for everything that was new in golf supplies.

His hobbies are horseback riding and farming.

175

*E.J. Smith was featured in the book Men of Achievement in the Carolinas by Leonard E. Johnson and Lloyd M. Smith, published by Men of Achievement, Inc., 1952.*

## Appreciation

# Smith Turf founder: Gentleman and friend

*By Michael J. Stott*

**B**y many accounts, Wayne B. Smith Sr., former chairman of the board of Charlotte, N.C.-based Smith Turf and Irrigation Co., was a generous man. He will be remembered by many throughout the Southeast as a gentleman and a pioneer in the golf course maintenance industry.

Smith, who was part of a business that was one of the oldest and largest Toro distributorships in the country, died Nov. 26 from complications following hip surgery. He was 93.

*Wayne B. Smith Sr.*

The company he founded is a leader in the outdoor power equipment industry, with 260 employees in four states and annual gross sales of more than $120 million. Its business segments include golf, sports fields and residential and commercial irrigation. In recent years the company has been run by Smith's sons, Wayne Jr. and Stephen, and is considered to have "an impeccable reputation in the region," said Trent Bouts, programs director for the Carolinas Golf Course Superintendents Association. "There is a reason they've been so successful for so long. They are really smart business people."

Part of the success is a lifelong commitment to customers.

"Wayne Sr. just set a standard with that company whereby it would always try to help golf courses and superintendents at every opportunity," said Bill Anderson, CGCS, director of greens and grounds at Carmel Country Club in Charlotte, where Smith was a former president.

In fact, the first meeting of the Carolinas GCSA was held at Carmel in 1953, so Smith "obviously supported superintendents from Day 1. He was repaid with a lot of loyalty and prospered," Anderson said.

Smith joined his father's organization, E.J. Smith Co., in 1933 and later served as its vice president.

"It was tough economic times for the industry back then," said Ray Avery, director of golf operations at The Club at Longview in Weddington, N.C., and former director of golf operations at Quail Hollow Country Club in Charlotte where Smith was a member.

"You'd hear that 'these are good people to work

*Wayne B. Smith Sr. (right) and his father, E.J. Smith (left), together during the 1950s.*

with.' There are all kinds of stories about that organization allowing people to pay them when they

could so they could stay in business."

For example, Smith often gave Carmel untold amounts of seed, fertilizer and equipment to keep it running when money was tight.

"The older generation might say without him the club may not have made it," Anderson said.

Clearly Carmel was not the only beneficiary. Smith's largesse was felt far and wide.

"He understood the business completely," Avery said.

E.J. Smith Co., an antecedent to Smith Turf, represented "everything you needed for the golf course industry including the golf shop," Avery said.

"He made an impact on other people's lives. His word was good. You could count on those guys to help you. They had tremendous generosity. That's the epitome of what that company was and still is today."

When Wayne Sr. and his brother, George, parted ways, splitting the business in 1985, Wayne choose to concentrate on the turf industry. From the beginning "he was the founder and leader of our company," said Bob Bell, Smith Turf's vice president and director of commercial sales and operations.

"He was absolutely the most fair and ethical man I've ever known. He insisted that everyone who worked for him perform in a professional manner," Bell said.

"He did a lot for employees and believed they were the company. The greatest thing he did was pass those qualities on to his sons and they still run the business that way."

In March 2000, Toro recognized Smith for 65 years of service, which included receipt of four Mr. Toro and/or Distributor of Excellence Awards (Toro's highest honors for distribution), four gold level awards and six best in division accolades.

Smith also was a lifetime member of the GCSAA and the Carolinas GCSA. In addition, he won the latter's Distinguished Service Award in 1994, and the Turfgrass Council of North Carolina presented him with its Eagles Award for being a leading mentor within the association.

*Contributing writer Michael J. Stott lives in Richmond, Va.*

*Article written by Michael J. Stott, published by the Virginia TurfGrass Association in 2006.*

# In Memory of Wayne B. Smith Sr. of Smith Turf & Irrigation Company

A true pioneer of the golf course maintenance industry in the Southeast, Wayne B. Smith Sr. passed away on November 26, 2006, at age 93. As chairman of the board of Smith Turf & Irrigation Company (the third-oldest distributor of Toro products in the U.S.), Mr. Smith and his sons had established the 260-employee company as one of the top 100 private companies in North Carolina and the turf industry's leading distributor in the nation.

The son of the late E.J. and Irene Smith, Wayne was born in 1913 in Minneapolis, Minnesota. The family moved to Jacksonville, Florida, where he graduated from Robert E. Lee High School and then attended the University of Alabama, where he was a member of the Pi Kappa Alpha fraternity. In 1933, he moved to Charlotte, North Carolina, where he joined his father at E.J. Smith Company. He went on to serve as vice president of E.J. Smith & Sons Company and then chairman of Smith Turf & Irrigation Company.

Mr. Smith was recognized by The Toro Company three times as its Distributor of Excellence, The Toro Company's highest award. He was a lifetime member of the Golf Course Superintendents Association of America (CGSAA), the Carolina Golf Course Superintendents Association (CGCSA) and the Turfgrass Council of North Carolina (TCNC), where he was presented with the prestigious Eagles Mentor Award as a leading mentor of the association.

Mr. Smith was a founding member of Avondale Presbyterian Church, as well as a founding member of Carmel Country Club in Charlotte, NC, where he served as the club's third president (the club's North Course is dedicated in his honor). Additionally, Wayne was a member of Quail Hollow Club in Charlotte, NC, and Hound Ears Club in Blowing Rock, NC.

Mr. Smith was a devoted and beloved father, grandfather and great grandfather. Preceded in death by his wife of 62 years, Lois Meacham Smith, Wayne is survived by three children, Wayne B. Smith Jr., and his wife Cindy; Stephen E. Smith, and his wife Tracy; Judy S. Martin, and her husband Dr. Edward S. Martin; and daughter-in-law Jonnie W. Smith; seven grandchildren and nine great-grandchildren.

Mr. Smith's true essence was in his character. His legacy is the countless number of people who were touched by his compassionate and caring heart and who admired him for his honesty, integrity, kindness and fairness. A generous and unpretentious man, he always put others first, and he was a generous donor to many charities and schools. It was often said that he was a small man with a very big heart and one of the world's great gentlemen.

The turf industry — and all who knew Mr. Smith — will greatly miss him, yet his example will live on in the hearts of family and friends alike.

*Wayne B. Smith Sr. was featured in an article in the Virginia Turfgrass Journal in 2007.*

*1933 Toro equipment*

*1937*

*1946*

*1961*

*1969*

*Wayne Smith Jr, Steve Smith, Anna-Lindsay Smith Yarbrough (behind, portraits of Wayne Smith Sr., and E.J. Smith)*

# ABOUT THE AUTHOR

Wayne Smith was born and raised in Charlotte, North Carolina, and educated at Myers Park High School and the University of North Carolina. He served in the US Air Force. He was a sales manager and later vice president of E.J. Smith & Sons Co., then president, chairman, and CEO of Smith Turf & Irrigation. He served on advisory boards and committees in the turfgrass industry. He served on the USGA Green Section Committee, the North Carolina Golf Panel, and was a commercial member of the Carolinas Golf Course Superintendents Association, where he received the Distinguished Service Award. He was chairman of the board of the Children's Theater of Charlotte, president of the Sportsman's Club of Charlotte, council vice president of the Charlotte Chamber of Commerce, served on the board of directors of the North Carolina Hall of Fame, served as a deacon in the Presbyterian Church, and was on the board of directors of the UNC Charlotte Athletic Foundation. He also served on a number of community organizations.

Married to Indun Patrick, Wayne has two daughters and five grandchildren.

Printed in the USA
CPSIA information can be obtained
at www.ICGtesting.com
LVHW072024121023
760591LV00091B/1116/J